The justification of the sinner in the world [has]
degenerated into the justification of sin and the world.
Costly grace was turned into cheap grace
without discipleship.
—*Dietrich Bonhoeffer*

The devil is a counterfeit artist who has distorted the biblical understanding of grace. If you miss the true meaning of grace, you will miss the doorway into God's supernatural and fall into serious error!

—*Sid Roth*
Host, *It's Supernatural!* TV

I stand with David Tomberlin and his understanding of grace in his new book, *Grace Is Free, but It Isn't Cheap*. It is a much-needed additional voice to the cheap grace that Bonhoeffer warned the church about in the 1940s while in prison before Hitler executed him for his involvement in the resistance. We need modern writers reminding us of the *cost of discipleship*, as Bonhoeffer did. Thank you, David, for reminding us of the dangers of the cheap-grace message.

—*Randy Clark*
President, Global Awakening Theological Seminary

I have known my friend David Tomberlin for almost two decades. I love his heart and complete dedication to bring the gospel to millions in the nations and his tenacity in pursuing the truth. I trust that as you read this book, you will be encouraged to embrace the truth, which, in turn, will cause you to know Jesus—the way, the truth, and the life—even better, more deeply, and more closely than ever before.

—*Mel Tari*
Author, *Like a Mighty Wind*
President and Founder, World Mission, Laguna Hills, CA

This book rightly divides the Word of truth about grace and addresses the error of "cheap grace" that has become rampant in the American church.

—*Joe Delgado*
Pastor, Christian Life Fellowship, Redlands, CA

DR. DAVID TOMBERLIN

GRACE
IS FREE, BUT IT
ISN'T CHEAP

CHALLENGING
TODAY'S WATERED-DOWN VERSION OF
CHRISTIANITY

WHITAKER
HOUSE

Unless otherwise indicated, all Scripture quotations are taken from the *Holy Bible, New International Version*®, NIV®, © 1973, 1978, 1984, 2011 by Biblica, Inc.® Used by permission. All rights reserved worldwide. The "NIV" and "New International Version" are trademarks registered in the United States Patent and Trademark Office by Biblica, Inc.® Scripture quotations marked (KJV) are taken from the King James Version of the Holy Bible. Scripture quotations marked (NKJV) are taken from the *New King James Version*®. Copyright © 1982 by Thomas Nelson. Used by permission. All rights reserved. Scripture quotations marked (NASB) are taken from the updated *New American Standard Bible*®, © 1960, 1971, 1977, 1995, 2020 by The Lockman Foundation. Used by permission. All rights reserved. (www.Lockman.org).

Boldface type in Scripture quotations indicates the author's emphasis.

Definitions of Hebrew and Greek words are taken from the electronic version of *Strong's Exhaustive Concordance of the Bible*, STRONG (© 1980, 1986, and assigned to World Bible Publishers, Inc. Used by permission. All rights reserved.).

GRACE IS FREE, BUT IT ISN'T CHEAP:
Challenging Today's Watered-Down Version of Christianity

David Tomberlin
www.DavidTomberlin.com
info@davidtomberlin.com

ISBN: 978-1-64123-903-5
eBook ISBN: 978-1-64123-904-2
Printed in the United States of America
© 2022 by David Tomberlin

Whitaker House
1030 Hunt Valley Circle
New Kensington, PA 15068
www.whitakerhouse.com

Library of Congress Control Number: 2022945944

1 2 3 4 5 6 7 8 9 10 11 ⨇ 29 28 27 26 25 24 23 22

DEDICATION

I would like to dedicate this book to my wife, Kate, whose love and support made this project possible; to Sam Farina, whose anointed prayer one night changed my entire life; to my awesome kids, who bring joy to me every day; to our friends and partners around the world who have held up my arms like Aaron and Hur held Moses's, empowering me to live out my calling; and to those who have, over the last twenty centuries—often against popular opinion—preached the message of the gospel without compromise. I am confident your reward shall never cease.

CONTENTS

Introduction: The Costliness of True Grace 11

1. When Greasy Grace Began 15

2. The Cotton-Candy Gospel 25

3. True Grace Versus Cheap Grace 41

4. Identifying the Fake Rolex of Theology 53

5. The Spread of the Snowflake Gospel 65

6. The Pendulum's Swing 81

7. Greasy Grace and Fake Holiness—
   Two Sides of the Same Bitcoin 99

8. Weeding Out the Telltale Talk of Cheap Grace 109

9. Getting Our Minds Right and Exposing
   the Enemy's Schemes 137

10. Agendas and Audiences 151

Conclusion: A Gospel About Nothing...or Everything 165

About the Author 173

INTRODUCTION:
THE COSTLINESS OF TRUE GRACE

Cheap grace [synonymous with greasy grace] *is the grace we bestow on ourselves. Cheap grace is the preaching of forgiveness without requiring repentance, baptism without church discipline, Communion without confession, absolution without personal confession. Cheap grace is grace without discipleship, grace without the cross, grace without Jesus Christ, living and incarnate.*
—Dietrich Bonhoeffer[1]

Dietrich Bonhoeffer, German pastor and theologian, stalwartly resisted the Nazis. He was imprisoned in 1943 and executed two years later. In the seven-plus decades since his

---

1. Dietrich Bonhoeffer, *The Cost of Discipleship* (New York: Macmillan, 1963), 47.

execution, his book *The Cost of Discipleship*, a compelling statement on the demands of sacrifice and moral consistency, continues to counter a secular society gone adrift. Bonhoeffer was only thirty-nine when he died, but he had already made a monumental contribution to Christian thought—a contribution that still has profound and growing significance today, in an age of cheap grace versus costly grace.

Cheap grace, greasy grace, sloppy agape, fake grace, the snowflake gospel (my addition to the collection of terms)... this 2,000-year-old theology goes by many names, but, in the end, it's all the same. Defined even more clearly, it is the gospel being preached as follows: "Of course, you have sinned; but now, everything is forgiven, so you can stay as you are and enjoy the consolations of forgiveness." The primary defect of such a proclamation is that it contains no demand for discipleship.

In contrast to this cheap grace, Bonhoeffer says, "Costly grace confronts us as a gracious call to follow Jesus, it comes as a word of forgiveness to the broken spirit and the contrite heart. Grace is costly because it compels a man to submit to the yoke of Christ and follow him; it is grace because Jesus says: 'My yoke is easy and my burden is light.'"[2] Bonhoeffer shifts the narrative for a moment from cheap grace to costly grace in his inimitable way.

> Such grace is *costly* because it calls us to follow, and it is *grace* because it calls us to follow *Jesus Christ*. It is costly because it costs a man his life, and it is grace because it gives a man the only true life. It is costly as it condemns sin, and grace because it justifies the sinner. Above all, it is *costly* because it cost God the life of his Son: "ye

were bought at a price," and what has cost God much cannot be cheap for us. Above all, it is *grace* because God did not reckon his Son too dear a price to pay for our life, but delivered him up for us. Costly grace is the Incarnation of God.[3]

Amazing grace, how sweet the sound…as the refrain of cheap grace dismantles it. Yet for anyone who takes the time to read the Bible without bias, cheap grace is quickly exposed for the scam that it is.

Throughout this book, we will identify the fallacies and platitudes of cheap grace and expose them for what they are. If you are offended at this point, I wrote this book for you. If you are excited about this topic and find it refreshing, I wrote this book for you. If you understand that there can be a space betwixt religious demagoguery and truth that brings freedom and life, I wrote this book for you.

I believe a gospel or a message from a preacher or thought leader should provoke and challenge our presuppositions. If you are someone who loves greasy grace and dares to take a second look at some of your ideologies, let's journey together in this offering. If you see through the fallacies of greasy grace and are seeking terminology and insights to help people you know to detox from this chicanery, let's journey together in this battle for truth. If you're simply interested in the topic and want to delve deeper into it, let's travel together in this offering.

One of the benefits of the time we live in is that a writer need not be disconnected from his audience. I hope you will feel free to respond, comment, and critique the thoughts in this book via

---

3. Bonhoeffer, *Cost of Discipleship*, 47–48.

our Facebook page and continue the dialogue. Let's experience "iron sharpening iron" (see Proverbs 27:17) as we pursue truth, knowledge, honesty, and, ultimately, the Lord Himself in a discussion of greasy grace and how it affects the church as well as the world at large.

In pursuit of true and lavish grace,
David Tomberlin

1

WHEN GREASY GRACE BEGAN

No one is immune from being lured into the trap of the mind trick practiced by cheap-grace preachers—even the most memorable and effective saints. In Matthew 16 (and in Mark 8, which relays the same story), Peter, the mighty apostle, had a momentary indiscretion of greasy grace that well may have been the earliest instance of the movement. He had just experienced a decisive moment with Jesus in which he received accolades and affirmations after giving a momentous response to Jesus's question *"Who do you say I am?"* (Matthew 16:15). Peter's revelation that Jesus was the Messiah led to a prophetic statement that Peter the rock would be foundational to building the church. He was probably on cloud nine. Unfortunately, his pride got the better of him, leading him to respond according to the flesh rather than the spirit.

Sometimes, our worst moments come right on the heels of our best moments. Peter went from being revelator of the year to receiving a very harsh correction. How did he slip into greasy grace? He objected to the Lord's prediction of His own death and suffering. (See Matthew 16:22.)

Lest we be tempted to give Peter a pass, thinking he had good intentions, Jesus's rebuke reveals otherwise. He told Peter, *"Get behind me, Satan!"* (Matthew 16:23). Peter, like many modern-day proponents of cheap grace, wanted to look like the "good guy." He tried to sound "nice" and "churchy." He wanted to be "positive." In Peter's mind, he was being helpful by defending Jesus, trying to protect and honor his friend. At least, that is what Peter thought he was doing. But Jesus knew better.

GOOD IDEAS VERSUS "GOD" IDEAS

Peter hoped to please the Lord. He had a good idea instead of a "God" idea, and by voicing it, he revealed how he was slipping into what is arguably the most demonic arena one can fall into—cheap grace.

Still, one can sympathize with Peter. He loved Jesus. He was having the time of his life, enjoying close and genuine fellowship with the Son of God. Yet despite this closeness, Peter had not learned that the kingdom of God operates differently than the kingdom of this world. When Jesus told Peter that He would suffer many things (see Matthew 16:21), Peter perceived it as a real downer and was probably wondering about the existence of a Plan B.

Undoubtedly, like all of us, Peter liked accolades and attention; he enjoyed the feeling that comes from winning and success. To be fair, who wouldn't? Suffering and death sounded like a loser's way out. Previously a rough-and-tumble fisherman, Peter had left everything he knew to follow Jesus, trading the daily drudgery of casting nets to masses of smelly fish for a brand-new life. His lot changed dramatically for the better. Now he was part of something impressive, part of a national movement. Peter was with the promised Messiah, and he knew it. No doubt it was beyond what he had ever dreamed of—witnessing miracles, ministering with the Messiah promised long ago by the prophets, and being in the inner circle, no less! His life had meaning, fame, and a daily supply of miraculous provision. He loved God, loved Jesus, and loved the way his life was going. He was living his "best life." So how could we blame him for resisting the idea of Jesus's death? Peter didn't want the good times to end.

And they weren't supposed to, according to Peter's understanding of the Messiah. The Messiah was expected to be a political/military figure who would overthrow the oppressive Roman government and restore dignity and glory to Israel. A lot of people would have called Peter crazy for taking up with a carpenter's son and believing He would push the oppressor's boot off their back. So, when Jesus started speaking of His imminent death, Peter couldn't handle it.

Even after the resurrection, the disciples were still under a wrongful impression of Jesus's intent. We see this in Acts 1:6, when they gathered around Him and asked, *"Lord, are you at this time going to restore the kingdom to Israel?"* As Bonhoeffer put it, "[T]he very notion of a suffering Messiah was a scandal to the Church, even in its earliest days. That is not the kind of Lord it wants, and as the Church of Christ it does not like to have the law of suffering imposed upon it by its Lord."[4]

On a less cynical note, Peter loved Jesus—his friend, his mentor, and his God. He had seen the miracles. He knew Jesus's sincerity and integrity. And he felt that his own success and future thriving were tied to those of his beloved Rabbi. He didn't want anything bad happening to Jesus, mainly because he loved Jesus but also because of his own self-interest. Nevertheless, the principles of God's kingdom don't change, even for the King.

One of the most profoundly difficult foundational principles of God's kingdom is that you have to die to live. (See, for example, John 12:24–25.) In God's kingdom, the first is last and the last is first (see Matthew 19:30; 20:16); you must serve to be great (see Mark 10:44); you must be willing to give up everything, that it might be given back to you in abundance (see Luke 6:38). Though you may weep for a night, joy comes in the morning. (See Psalm 30:5.)

These are hard things to understand in our culture, and they're even harder to embrace and live out. They seem counterintuitive, hence the reason some people—even good, well-meaning people like Peter—get tripped up by greasy grace. It does seem right, in a way, and it appeals to our human nature to avoid pain at all costs. Yet that was never part of what Jesus died to give us.

Cheap grace is dangerous because it is deceptive. It feels right on so many levels, which is the basis of deception. It's a

4. Bonhoeffer, *Cost of Discipleship*, 96.

cunningly crafted lie; it's evil that seems reasonable. The gospel minus the cross of Christ—an easy road, a primrose path—presents itself as benevolent, beneficial, and "right." Today's Christian churches, pulpits, and pews alike are filled with "good guys" avoiding unpleasant or painful truths for a variety of reasons. Some are making honest mistakes; others have more devious aims. In the end, it's all the same—absolutely destructive.

> GREASY GRACE APPEALS TO OUR HUMAN NATURE TO AVOID PAIN AT ALL COSTS, YET THAT WAS NEVER PART OF WHAT JESUS DIED TO GIVE US.

In Peter's case, I think it's essential for us to recognize that his slip was not intentional. Many "greasy-gracers" have good intentions, but they do not have God's concerns in mind, but merely human concerns, as Peter did. (See Matthew 16:23.)

A BITTER PILL TO SWALLOW

I once heard a preacher say, "The problem with a living sacrifice is that it keeps wiggling off the altar." In God's kingdom, death comes before resurrection. No death means no life; it is a bitter pill but an important one.

Sometimes, we step in stuff, and we are the last to smell it. Two thousand years later, the same demonic concept of "sacrifice nothing" spirit is operating. Greasy-grace preachers and proponents feel they are doing Jesus a favor by saying, "Jesus, we don't want You to look bad, sound mean, or come across as controversial. We've got You covered. We're going to change what You say to make You look better and be more presentable. What You're offering? Death? Well, that just doesn't sell, so we'll reword Your offer as something more palatable. Trust us, Jesus, You'll get more YouTube views, Facebook likes, and Instagram followers."

Such adjustments to the words and actions of Jesus can be seen across the board in the greasy-grace camp when anything costly, problematic, or challenging is addressed. "Jesus, You said we should fast, but how about this: we aren't fasting. You said, 'Die to live,' but we're going with 'Jesus paid it all'! You don't need to die to live! See how good we're making You look, Jesus? Aren't You glad You got off that whole 'death' thing? Jesus, You said, *'Wide is the gate and broad is the road that leads to destruction...but small is the gate and narrow the road that leads to life, and* **only a few find it***'* (Matthew 7:13–14). This sounds just a teensy bit close-minded, Jesus. Let's just say that You are so 'good,' and You didn't really mean what You said in that dusty ol' Bible. How about that? You'll sound a lot more progressive that way. Oh, and let's throw out all this talk of people being thrown into hell, *'where the fire never goes out'* (Mark 9:43), meaning eternal fire and punishment. We focus-grouped that one. Major downer. How about this: when You died on the cross, Your blood covered all sin. Like a 'finished work,' but not in the sense of making it available to anyone; everyone gets it just for being born, no matter what they do! It's like free trophies for everyone! You will look good; people will feel good. Jesus, it's a win-win." Like cheap shoe salesmen, greasy-grace preachers rattle on. They rationalize that a "loving God" couldn't have meant all that "mean" stuff, so we should just tidy it up a bit, making it more saleable, more palatable.

Just as Peter tried to talk Jesus down off the cross, so too do the cheap-grace preachers of today try to talk Christians down off the cross that Jesus instructed them to take up. (See Matthew 16:24; Mark 8:34.)

JESUS SAYS, BUT WHAT SAY YOU?

Jesus says we must die to ourselves to live, take up our cross, follow Him, and fast and pray. He also instructed us to tithe and take care of widows and orphans. Do you remember when He said that the greatest would be the servant of all? (See Mark 9:35.) Jesus said that anyone who would inherit eternal life must eat of His flesh and drink of His blood. (See John 6:51, 53–58.)

But the adherents of the greasy-grace gospel will have none of it. Like self-indulgent adult children ordering an Oreo smoothie from their mom while living in her basement, they cry out, "Jesus paid it all, so I don't have to do anything. Now where is my Oreo smoothie?" Entitled and enabled by those around them, they expect to get everything without having to give—or give up—anything. In effect, they say, "God's love is so good that He has no standards, and the Bible doesn't mean what it says about the requirement of living a pure life." In other words, "Jesus died so I could live my life in the flesh."

This group uses the blood of Jesus as an excuse to do what they want instead of as motivation and empowerment to do what God wants. They mock the work Jesus did on the cross and pervert its meaning and intent. It's the same group that calls perversion "love," the same group that calls sin "good" because it's "covered by the blood of Jesus." This group honors God with their lips but denies His power to transform. They're the group of whom God says, *"These people honor me with their lips, but their hearts are far from me. They worship me in vain; their teachings are merely human rules"* (Matthew 15:8–9; see also Isaiah 29:13). They prioritize their theologies—philosophies and teachings of man.

> GREASY-GRACERS USE THE BLOOD OF JESUS
> AS AN EXCUSE TO DO WHAT THEY
> WANT INSTEAD OF AS MOTIVATION AND
> EMPOWERMENT TO DO WHAT GOD WANTS.

Oh, sure, they will tell you that they have more faith because they believe Jesus's "finished work" was greater than anything one could imagine. "You just don't understand 'grace'!" they shout as they figuratively lean against their bookshelf full of participation medals.

Peter felt the same way. "Why should You suffer, Jesus?" he essentially asked. "Why should You die? We have a good thing going. I love You. I don't want anything to happen to You." In truth, these people don't want anything to happen to them, but they position the words in such a fashion to make themselves look heroic and enlightened.

They have bought into the false framework of greasy grace, a permutation of the gospel that seems sweet but, in the end, fails to satisfy. It was these people Jude was talking about when he wrote, *"For certain individuals whose condemnation was written about long ago have secretly slipped in among you. They are ungodly people, who pervert the grace of our God into a license of immorality and deny Jesus Christ our only Sovereign and Lord"* (Jude 1:4).

2

THE COTTON-CANDY GOSPEL

Kids love cotton candy for its sweet flavor and fun texture. But when the sugar rush is over, you are left with no benefit—no nutritional value whatsoever. Greasy grace could easily be called a "cotton-candy gospel." It tastes good at first but makes you feel sick in your spirit later.

As a boy growing up in Alvin, Texas, I remember fondly the times when a carnival would come through town. These carnivals were...how can I put it? They were "dressed down," so to speak—simple, fun, unpretentious, and, to be fair, a teensy bit on the trashy side, but in a good way.

Carnivals put on full display the practice of cutting corners to address budgetary concerns. For example, maintenance costs of the tilt-a-whirl were clearly viewed as optional. Replace the parts? Pish-posh. A little WD-40 and some duct tape were all that a country boy needed to keep things running right. In our community, they called it "Southern engineering." In Texas in the 80s, safety wasn't the highest priority.

Inevitably, a curious cast of characters worked at these temporary, traveling diversions. There was the proverbial one-armed carny running a squeaky, metallic carnival ride who, in a feat of masterful dexterity, simultaneously smoked a cigarette, tore apart red entry tickets, and ushered kids on and off the ride, all with his good arm. While we waited in line, he might also entice us with a colorful, profanity-laced tale of his tour in Vietnam, back then known as "Nam." The carnival workers were traveling men, never overly enthusiastic, hygienic, mannered, or distinguished. Lights, rides, bugs, food, games, and copious amounts of liquified nacho cheese filled the atmosphere. Outsiders might have found it a bit on the sketchy side, but we loved it.

Along with rides, there were plenty of games of chance. If you played and won, you got a prize. To be sure, these games did not have a high probability of success. For example, "knock down three pins with a bean bag and win a prize" seemed like a useless scam, even to my eight-year-old self. I always wondered who could possibly get suckered into playing it. From the one-armed carnies to the scam games, there were plenty of life lessons to be learned in such an environment.

One reason such carnivals were well attended in the town where I grew up is that we didn't have tons of other things to do. The local Sonic drive-in, cow tipping, shooting out streetlights, and mailbox baseball composed most of the options for evening entertainment.

To paint the picture of my surroundings, my buddy John was a celebrated member of our school and also our football team. His accolades were not due to his skill with the venerated pigskin or his academic prowess. He seldom played, mostly sitting on the bench in football, and struggled to pass his classes. He wasn't particularly charismatic or overly talented. He was just well-loved and esteemed because of his father, who liked to drive around our little Texas town in his lavishly painted blue truck, speakers blaring country music, a fully grown Bengal tiger in a cage in the truck bed. This was *Tiger King*, 80s Texas version, albeit less "flamboyant," if you catch my meaning. In our little town, you wouldn't find any fancy people, but you could see tigers riding in truck beds, an exhibit of alligators in the lobby of the local bank, and, at one point, even a bar featuring a beer-drinking buffalo. For a dollar fifty, patrons could purchase a beer for the buffalo and then watch the enchanting beast enjoy a round right from the bottle. Buster III was his name, and he could drink an entire case in one standing.

Not exactly "one with nature," we enjoyed the spectacle of more dangerous animals. We had no high-end shopping malls, luxury auto dealerships, or other standard metropolitan offerings. Fancy? No. Interesting place and people? Without question.

So, whenever a carnival came to town, offering rides and games, we welcomed it like a long-lost friend. My brothers and I always rolled up our sleeves and got right into the shenanigans at these events.

"LOVE" THAT ISN'T HEALTHY

One problem at these carnivals was the intersection of too many unhealthy dining options and our family's limited discretionary funds budget. My insatiable appetite for sugar compounded this problem, creating many conflicts between my parents and me at such events. I remember one occasion when I asked my mom for another cotton candy, candied apple, funnel cake, or whatever high-ranking glycemic index item I was after.

She said, "No, you've had enough."

She was right, no question, but I was disheartened. The lights were swirling, music playing, and the love bugs fraternizing, but I was losing my sugar buzz. I had been shut down.

Just then, I looked over to my left. There stood a chubby kid with a helium balloon strapped to his wrist. He wore a silver necklace and some designer clothes that were definitely better than the hand-me-downs I was used to. In one hand was an ice cream cone; in the other was a big lollipop of swirled blue, pink, and white that looked like it could last for days. Blue syrup from the lollipop ran down the boy's cheek while ice cream dripped down his hand. The Texas heat, even at night, was merciless toward frozen treats. His doting mother waited for him to chew the chili-cheese dog she quasi force-fed him between slurps of ice cream and licks of lollipop, all the while urging him, "Eat, my son! Eat!"

Even as a young kid, I could see this was not the right way to "love" someone. Don't get me wrong. I was still jealous. *Some kids have all the luck,* I thought. *Cool clothes, a shiny necklace, a doting mom, and more unhealthy food than a kid could dream of. Oh, to be that boy for just one night!*

Still, deep down, I knew that what was happening with the kid wasn't healthy. I was torn. Even with my unapologetic appreciation for all things sugar related, I knew that mother's liberality would lead to trouble for her kid in the future. It was not a good long-term strategy, and I could see as much with my jealous eyes, even as I longed for just one bite of that gorgeous chili-cheese dog.

It's highly possible that this young mother was like so many other parents who faced hunger and lack in their growing-up years and determined that their own children would never experience the same—often going above and beyond meeting their children's needs to the point of insisting their kids eat big all the time. Such parents probably couldn't have afforded to attend carnivals in their youth, and they wanted to make sure their own kids enjoy every possible indulgence.

Whatever her motives, anyone could see this mother had a sweet and loving heart. And yet, in spite of her good intentions in spoiling her son, what she was doing would only harm him in the long run.

THE FOLLY OF GREASY GRACE

I can easily envision that kid at forty-five years of age, having struggled his whole life with weight problems and a sugar addiction. Or maybe he fought the patterns of his childhood diet and now hosts a health and fitness program on Instagram. Either of these outcomes would have been the result of the "love" his mom gave him—whether going along with it or struggling to break free of that pattern.

The doting, pampering, and force-feeding of chili-cheese dogs *seemed* like love, but it was an albatross. This situation presents a living analogy of greasy grace—something that sounds or looks good but ultimately leads to destruction. Those who promote such a "gospel" may well have sincere intentions, but their judgment is in question.

A similar story, a bit closer to home, came from a conversation I had with my maternal grandfather regarding a way he had of "loving" his family that actually enfeebled them in a crucial area. Before I get to that part, though, I need to give you some background. My grandfather's life started very humbly. He grew up during the Depression in a family of subsistence farmers in Anson, Texas. His childhood home, ordered from a Sears catalog, had the rare distinction of boasting an indoor bathroom. It was the envy of his neighbors, none of whom could afford such a luxury.

Rising at daybreak to milk the cows and collect eggs for breakfast, then picking cotton before and after school, he dreamed of a better life. There wasn't any irrigation system in West Texas, so the only water their crops received came from the rain. This was known as dryland farming, and it was by no means a profitable venture. If it rained, there would be a crop generating a modest income. If it didn't rain...well, you get the picture. My grandfather told me that the family's annual income once dipped as low as $75. (To put things in perspective, the average middle-class family would have earned about $1,000 per year at that time.) Fortunately for my grandfather's family, living off the land kept them from going hungry. It was a simple yet hard way of life, and the struggle made my grandfather determined to be successful. He didn't want to spend his life just squeaking by as a farmer.

His ticket to success was a natural athletic ability honed by years of hard physical labor. He earned a full football scholarship to McMurry University, becoming the first in his family to go to college. At eighteen years of age, he left his family farm with just five dollars in his pocket and headed off for his freshman year.

It was in college that he met my grandmother. The daughter of a Methodist circuit-riding preacher, she had grown up in a highly conservative home. To her dying day, she never swam or wore a bathing suit. The Methodists back then were of the "holiness camp," and the very idea of a Methodist preacher's daughter wearing a swimsuit was unthinkable.

When my grandmother arrived at university at age sixteen, she was the belle of the ball, with beauty, propriety, and a singing voice like an angel's. And upon being crowned university football queen—the highest social honor a female student could achieve at the time—she was duly viewed the most desirable bachelorette on campus.

My grandfather excelled in his scholastic efforts and in sports alike and was elected captain of the football team. He also lettered in basketball and baseball. He was an accomplished athlete to the point that I had the privilege, years later, of being with him when he was inducted into his university's sports hall of fame.

In his university time, he was coupled with my grandmother, the classy and beautiful football queen and stand-out singer. It was classic Americana served in 1940s style, and he was doing well, sending money back home that he had earned working the night shift at a Coca-Cola bottling plant. Both he and my grandmother had grown up in poverty but had been raised with a solid foundation of morality and ethics, and at university, their good habits began to pay off.

A SKEWED WAY OF SHOWING LOVE

My grandfather's education took a detour when he shipped out to Europe for a few years to fight in World War II in the middle of his university years. Just before leaving, he married my grandmother, the love of his life, knowing there was a reasonable chance he wouldn't make it back to her. The war was brutal, and he didn't talk about it much, other than to joke that he'd gotten to see Europe on a free tour paid for by the government. Anytime I asked him about it, I always got a short answer—the kind of answer that indicated he'd rather not discuss it.

I can only imagine how miserable it must have been for a farm boy from West Texas to camp out in the cold and snow in leaky tents, living on K rations and knowing he or one of his friends could be killed at any moment. Danger in the air, chaos everywhere, missing home and waiting weeks or even months for returned written correspondence...the emotional toll was tough. Even for those who believed in the war and knew the importance of what they were doing, such motives of nobility and honor could prop them up emotionally for only so long.

Being a good Southern Baptist, my grandfather never smoked or drank, except as part of a southern remedy for the flu. A little Wild Turkey whiskey, lemon juice, and hot water with a side of Vicks VapoRub would cure whatever ailed you. So, as a nonsmoking, alcohol-abstaining Baptist, he would sell his army-rationed cartons of cigarettes and use the money to buy Parisian perfume for my grandmother.

The Allies celebrated the war's end in the fall of 1945, but France had a long road to recovery ahead. The nation had been bombed to a pile of rubble by the Germans, and there were shortages everywhere. Many French girls were reduced to selling their bodies for a can of Coke or a candy bar. Despite many a PSA given to the soldiers about the dangers of promiscuity, many soldiers received forever souvenirs in the form of incurable STDs. Other soldiers made a sport of riding around Paris in their army Jeeps, tossing partially smoked cigarettes into the street and laughing as they watched groups of desperate French people fighting over them for the remaining puffs.

While many of his compatriots were entertaining themselves at the expense of the French, my grandfather and some of his fellow soldiers gave another two or three years of their lives to help rebuild the nation. When he finally came home, it was with a new, keener understanding of suffering—and a commitment to keep his own family from having to suffer. He knew what it was like to go without, to be hungry, to be uncomfortable, and to see death all around. He didn't want that for his family.

He returned to Abilene and finished his bachelor's degree, the first in his family to do so. After graduation, he started working as a football coach and teacher. He earned his master's degree in education and became an administrator and, eventually, a principal of a large high school in the famous cattle town of Amarillo, Texas, where he was responsible for the educational needs of more than 3,000 students. During his years there, he helped his school navigate the messy process of desegregation and hired the town's first African American vice principal—a man whom he treated like family. One time, my grandfather was at a restaurant with the Black vice principal and several other White school staff members when the owner said, "You gentlemen are welcome, but he"—pointing at the vice principal—"cannot eat here." My grandfather replied, "If he goes, we all go," and the group got up and walked out.

In those days, his stance was not considered heroic, but he didn't care. He was a stand-up guy who did what he knew was right. But, despite his strong moral compass, when it came to raising my mom, Pawpaw fell into a similar trap as the mother at the carnival. Like most people who grew up with little, he wanted to give his kids all the luxuries he never enjoyed. Whatever my mom wanted, he would buy for her, and he was constantly giving her spending money.

I remember my mom saying that he would stuff her purse with tens and twenties anytime she went out. He always wanted to make sure she "had enough." A wonderful sentiment, to be sure, but, in my mom's case, it was also eventually debilitating.

My mom told me that she would sometimes discover hundreds of dollars in the bottom of her purse. Remember, this was Texas in the 1950s and 60s, when a hamburger cost a dime, maybe 15 cents. A new car cost less than $3,000. Today's equivalent would be a teenage girl finding a few thousand dollars in her purse.

It was too much. It was over-the-top.

Every father wants to take care of his daughter, as he should. One way of doing this is to teach responsibility, sound money management, and a good work ethic. Unfortunately, my mom was never taught these lessons, and she and my dad ended up in a state of financial dependence on my grandfather.

My grandfather's attempt to love his daughter, in his mind, compensated for what he felt was missing in his own life. Giving so much to my mom created problems and eventually made her a lifelong dependent, leading to a dysfunctional relationship.

Growing up, money troubles were a constant source of friction in our family. Resentment manifested when my grandfather would give my parents money and then complain about how they were managing it. He would swear that he would never give them another cent, but this always amounted to an empty threat.

It was unending. My grandfather would sometimes vent to us grandkids with my parents in earshot. "What kind of grown man would need to ask his in-laws for money? Nobody did that for me!" he'd say. Or, "I took care of myself and my family as a man should! I used to work a second job, and even when I was a teacher, I took the bus! I didn't have a car handed to me. Money doesn't grow on trees! A man should be responsible for his family."

Such statements were unapologetic digs at my father, who, not one for conflict, always remained silent. It was an ugly scene that would replay itself year after year, almost as if the aroma of roasting turkey or the sight of the shimmering tinsel on the Christmas tree subconsciously triggered a discussion on responsibility with personal finances.

CAUGHT IN THE MIDDLE

On some level, I could see where my grandfather was coming from. I agreed that a man should take care of his family and be responsible. And yet, without question, anyone can experience temporary hardship and find themselves in need of a hand. However, being in need of a hand *all* the time is probably a dysfunction that should be addressed. While I understood and agreed with my grandfather's overall point, I did not appreciate the disrespect he directed at my dad. Being caught in the middle, I felt torn.

It was like this all my life. About the time I finished university and was starting graduate school, I had heard enough. On that day, it was just my grandfather and I in his backyard. My grandfather, whom I loved and respected a great deal, went on one of his regular rants. He had just sent some money to my parents, and he was livid.

"What's wrong with these people? They are grown and still can't manage their money? Don't they have any self-respect? Why don't they get another job? A man needs to work hard! Why do I always keep them afloat? Nobody helped me."

Suddenly, I'd had enough. It felt like all the years I had been stuck in the middle of that conversation had mounted up in a crushing tidal wave I couldn't restrain. I didn't believe in talking back to my elders, but I'd had all I could take.

I turned, looked him right in the eye, and said, firmly but respectfully, "You created this problem. You enabled them. You never kicked them out of the nest so they could grow their wings and fly. I love you, Pawpaw, but this is your fault. You gave them money all their life and never let them fight for it. You created dependents."

He looked at me sternly and was quiet for a moment. Then he blurted out, "*What* was I supposed to do? Let them go on *welfare?*" In my grandfather's eyes, going on welfare was just a little worse than dying. My grandfather is the kind of person who would rather go hungry and homeless than accept food stamps or go on welfare.

His invoking the welfare concept was a strong play, but I had an answer. "They *are* on welfare," I told him. "They're on *your* welfare! It's not the government, but it's the same thing."

He got quiet.

"If you want to give them something, that's your business. But you created this problem. Don't complain about it now!"

In a moment of begrudging but necessary reflection, he looked me in the eye and sighed. "You know what? I guess you're right."

It was an odd moment. My grandfather was not one to always need to be right or to have the last word, but he wouldn't concede a point unless he meant it.

We never broached the subject again.

THE TRAP OF FALSE LOVE

What this saga taught me was that "love" can't be just a good intention. Love has to be *strategic* because true love requires the effort to be well thought out. Love has to walk in wisdom. Tough love is better than sloppy agape. Real love and connectedness require something from both parties.

When love is given, then there must be a response.

Greasy grace that enables dysfunctional behavior isn't love at all. On the surface, it may appear like love, or an intention to love. But when you dig deeper, you see that it's a perversion of love, a misguided attempt.

GREASY GRACE THAT ENABLES DYSFUNCTIONAL BEHAVIOR ISN'T LOVE AT ALL.

This broken form of false love is personified by the stereotypical emotionally broken and fragile wife of the alcoholic. She trembles as she cracks another beer and delivers it to her always-angry-unless-drunk husband. He's already had too many, but she convinces herself she is doing this for love. "This is what he likes; it makes him feel better," she tells herself. "He won't be so angry if he has a few more. I'm helping keep the peace in our house."

In reality, she isn't doing it for love. She's enabling his destructive behavior, knowingly or unknowingly, for her own benefit. Like the cheap-grace preacher, she gets uncomfortable around conflict. Safe spaces are what she longs for. She knows what her husband is like when she doesn't keep the beers coming. Early in their relationship, she foolishly brought up the idea of setting limits on alcohol consumption, and he made sure she paid for her mistake.

For the average woman in this type of situation, it's probably a familiar scene. Her dad was likely also an alcoholic. Her mom no doubt modeled how to approach the dilemma of being a vulnerable wife and taught her that keeping the cold ones coming was the best way to avoid conflict.

Fitness coach Jonathan Mead, at uncagedhuman.com, helps clients erase the dysfunctional approaches they've been following in order to open up a new, healthy path. According to Mead, "Sometimes the easiest way to solve a problem is to stop participating in the problem."[5] This wisdom proves just as relevant when we're wondering how to love people without contributing to their dysfunction.

When we "love" the wrong way or operate in greasy grace, we are participating in the lie, thereby enabling dysfunction. A lot of the time, dysfunction is a learned behavior where fear often masquerades itself as love. Looking deeper, what looks like "love" to the casual observer is sometimes discovered to be a fear-based move of self-preservation. And it's this kind of "love" that underlies all proponents of greasy grace.

This is the folly of greasy grace, like Peter attempting to talk Jesus down from the cross and, therefore, His destiny. When someone tries to do good in the flesh, it almost always turns out bad in the end. Why do they do it? Because of warped love, lack of insight, poverty of wisdom, and shallow understanding. In the coming chapters, we will unpack how people come to subscribe to greasy grace—and how to avoid being among them.

---

5. Jonathan Mead, Motivation.com, http://www.motivation.com/quotes/1162.

3

TRUE GRACE VERSUS CHEAP GRACE

*The first duty of the gospel preacher is to declare God's law
and show the nature of sin.*
—Martin Luther

*I do not believe that any man can preach the gospel who
does not preach the Law.*
—Charles Spurgeon

*Before I can preach love, mercy, and grace, I must preach
sin, Law, and judgment.*
—John Wesley

So far, we have gotten an idea of what constitutes greasy grace—a "cotton-candy" gospel that tastes sweet but has no substance, no depth. It's a twisted form of love that is devoid of truth and wisdom. It's the pyrite—fool's gold—of love. It's fake "good" news. Those with wisdom and a real relationship with the Lord know the difference.

To understand true grace, we must understand the nature of true love. Today, in cultures across the world, many twisted and perverted ideas about love prevail. In our vernacular speech, "love" is often really just perversion, with people refusing to hold others accountable for sin, lest they hurt that person's feelings. Many people have confused love with permissiveness, going on to accept that which God rejects and to buy in to lies and falsehoods in order to coddle the emotions of another. This deception runs deep in the Western church, and it must be directly challenged and rectified.

In contrast to perverted "love," authentic love is commitment, devotion, honor, sacrifice for another, and honesty. In 1 Thessalonians 2, the apostle Paul exemplifies sincere love rather than a corrupted imitation when he confronts and corrects the Thessalonians while also describing and demonstrating his love for them. In verses seven and eight, Paul uses the analogy of a nursing mother caring for her child. It was never Paul's intention to impose a financial burden on the church, so he performed manual labor, working day and night at a secular job. He put the church's needs above his own needs. Often, sometimes unknowingly, preachers of greasy grace promote own their needs for attention and acceptance above the church's need for the truth.

LOVE DOES THE HARD THING

To Paul, love meant getting the job done without seeking attention for himself. He expressed his love for the people he served through genuine care. He explains his heartfelt affection for the church with language we can relate to. His description invokes what is probably nature's clearest example of love—a nursing mother giving her heart, as well as her body, to her young child. The internal feelings of devotion and care are expressed outwardly by the giving of herself to another, not just with deep affection but also with the sacrifice of time and physical effort.

As I was writing this book, my wife, Kate, was nursing our daughter Rachel. Rachel was such a happy baby who still smiles almost nonstop and likes to dance around as she laughs. And yet taking care of her, as a seven-month-old, required a lot of work. While I slept comfortably, my wife would be waking at three in the morning to nurse the baby, giving her life, nourishment, and a feeling of connectedness and warmth. I'm sure it isn't fun to wake up at three a.m. to feed a crying baby, but that's what love does. Love does the hard thing.

LOVE ALSO SAYS THE HARD THING

We have a table aquarium in our living room. Little Rachel loves to crawl over and look at the fish in the tank. She can sit there for quite a long time. She also likes to pull herself up and bang on the glass, which is not only terrible for the fish but also makes us concerned that she could hurt herself. When Rachel does this or engages in another activity of questionable safety, such as getting close to an electrical cord or chewing someone's shoe, my wife quickly puts a stop to it—sometimes with a vehemence that startles or upsets little Rach. Is Kate a killjoy seeking to steal her daughter's joy or toy with her emotions? Of course not. At this age, does Rachel understand the potential dangers of some of her behaviors? Does she know it's wrong to bang on a fish tank or eat shoes? Not yet. Rachel doesn't like it when her mom speaks forcefully or disciplines her, even though these things are done for her own good.

Paul's analogy in 1 Thessalonians morphs into a loving father's care for, and discipline of, his children, which extends to all ages, when Paul says, *"For you know that we dealt with each of you as a father deals with his own children, encouraging, comforting and urging you to live lives worthy of God"* (1 Thessalonians 2:11–12). The idea, of course, is spiritual growth to maturity—and this becomes possible only when we are willing to submit to, and offer, godly admonitions. The goal is for us to…

> …*reach unity in the faith and in the knowledge of the Son of God and become mature…. Then we will no longer be infants, tossed back and forth by the waves, and blown here and there by every wind of teaching and by the cunning and craftiness of people in their deceitful scheming. Instead,* **speaking the truth in love***, we will grow to become in every respect the mature body of him who is the head, that is, Christ.* (Ephesians 4:13, 14–15)

Love—real, genuine love—doesn't always tell you what you want to hear. Love will risk upsetting someone in order to help them avoid danger and stay safe. Love does what's *right*, not what's wanted. Love corrects sinful behaviors and attitudes, for even *"the* LORD *disciplines those he loves, as a father the son he delights in"* (Proverbs 3:12). Love is strong enough to risk the relationship so that truth can remain. Sometimes, love is tough and even unpleasant.

True grace makes room for tough love, including those challenging biblical passages that confront your accustomed theologies. Explaining such passages away is not in the purview of true grace. Authentic grace cannot exist apart from those potentially distasteful and demanding truths—the truths that can set you free. The juxtaposition of God's love and judgment must be maintained if there is to be integrity of thought combined with honest biblical reflection and interpretation. Actual grace is not a feel-good, cotton-candy treat. Real grace has spiritual nutrients, vitamins to build healthy attitudes, protein to build muscle of faith in the Word, and antioxidants to ward off the cancer of sin. Real grace might not launch you into a sugar high like cotton candy, but it will strengthen you, equip you, heal you, and help you grow into maturity and fulfill your calling.

Recently, while doing an in-depth study of the book of Matthew, I noticed that Jesus had a lot of hard things to say. At least nine times, He warned His hearers about the horrors of hell and went on to say, *"Wide is the gate and broad is the road that leads to destruction, and many enter through it"* (Matthew 7:13).

The idea that many people are headed for an eternity in hell, where *"the fire is not quenched"* (Mark 9:48), is not a pleasant one. Many of our friends, family members, coworkers, and even fellow church members may be damned and punished for eternity, and that thought is far from comforting. Quite the contrary, it is perhaps the saddest and most sobering truth there is. Yet grace does not exist outside of truth, and it will tell us the hard, true thing. Grace warns people of their impending judgment, God's wrath, and their eventual punishment in eternity if they continue in disobedience. Skimming past such verses and downplaying them doesn't help. The church needs to awaken from the lulling song of greasy grace and face the music of the words of Jesus.

AUTHENTIC GRACE LEADS TO REPENTANCE AND FORGIVENESS

Real grace brings the hope that true biblical understanding alone can introduce. When we understand true grace, we know that God made a way for the worst of sinners. Grace says that no matter what you have done, forgiveness is available to you. However, this forgiveness only comes if you turn from your evil ways and embrace Christ's work on the cross through faith.

The choice is for the hearers to make. They can embrace Christ, finding His forgiveness and the promise of eternal life, or die in their sins and face eternal punishment. People who love and understand verifiable grace don't fall short of the reality and importance of this message. When you know true grace, you can understand why greasy grace is not just erroneous but also *demonic*. It's a counterfeit substitute of true grace and, therefore, an enemy of God and an insult to the cross. As Bonhoeffer wrote, "Cheap grace is the deadly enemy of our Church."[6]

Greasy grace isn't just a harmless footnote of a well-intended teacher who has neglected proper study. Much like the Pharisees in Jesus's day, it fools people into thinking they are right with God when they are not. It is the cruelest of scams and the darkest of lies. It pats people on the back, assuring them of safety, as they haplessly walk down the road toward their eternal destruction and doom. It is the most unloving and ungracious thing one can preach.

---

6. Bonhoeffer, *Cost of Discipleship*, 45.

Once we have come to understand what real love is, we have to learn how to love—really love. Not enabling. Not being motivated by the praises of man, but loving our hearers enough to tell the difficult truth when it's called for.

GREASY GRACE IS THE MOST UNLOVING AND UNGRACIOUS THING ONE CAN PREACH.

Jesus never had a problem doing this. His time on earth was short. His life and ministry were eternally impactful, but they were brief. He didn't have time for games. He spoke the truth. He didn't care if the Pharisees liked it and didn't care if His hearers liked it. He didn't care if His disciples liked it. He didn't care about the opinions of men. His job was to please the Father, love the Father, and express that love by doing the Father's will, which often meant confronting people with the truth.

"FOR YOUR OWN GOOD" DOESN'T ALWAYS FEEL GOOD

I once heard the story about a busy minister who had to take his young son to the doctor for a booster shot. The minister was so busy that he arranged with the pediatrician to meet him early in the morning to give his son the shot before regular office hours started. Typically, there would have been a nurse or another type of assistant there to help administer the shot and, if need be, hold the patient down so the shot could be given appropriately. Because of the early hour, no other staff was on hand; the pediatrician was the sole practitioner present. And this pediatrician asked the boy's father to hold his son during the shot.

The father agreed and took hold of his son, who began to grow nervous. This behavior wasn't normal for his dad. He watched in alarm as the doctor approached him with a strange, sharp-looking object. *Who is this strange man coming at me with this scary object?* he wondered to himself. *And why is Dad holding me so firmly? He doesn't normally do this. He is usually caring and loving, looking out for my best interests. Just yesterday, he was playing with me, and last Saturday, he bought me ice cream.*

As the doctor came closer, the boy began to scream. How could he possibly understand what his father meant when he said, "Hold still, son. This will only be painful for a moment. And it's for your own good. I'm doing this because I love you"?

The boy's expression as he screamed was one of shock, betrayal, and bewilderment. "Why, Dad? Don't you love me? Ow! That hurts so much! I'm bleeding! What's happening? Why are you doing this to me?"

As outsiders observing a scene such as this, we can be emotionally removed and reasonable. We know that shots are moments of temporary discomfort for a long-term benefit. But the boy couldn't see things that way. He felt pain, betrayal, fear, terror. It was the worst experience of his life that he could remember. The observer or hearer of this story has the benefit of emotional detachment, but the boy's experience and the related feelings were real to him in the moment.

How hard this must have been for the father, and how hard it is for any of us, as parents, to subject our children to unpleasant experiences that are meant to help them in the long run. This minister loved his son with all his heart. He didn't want him to hurt or to doubt his dad's loyalty for even a second. He would have happily given his life for his son, and the look of fear and betrayal on his boy's face was unbearable. Even though he knew he was doing the right thing, it still pained him.

IT ISN'T EASY TILL IT'S OVER

The Bible is full of stories about people who had to endure temporary pain and hardship for their ultimate good. I'm sure Joseph didn't understand why God allowed him to be enslaved and imprisoned in Egypt until the outcome became clear, and he was able to say to his brothers, "*You intended to harm me, but God intended it for good to accomplish what is now being done, the saving of many lives*" (Genesis 50:20). And when David was leading his men against the Amalekites in Ziklag, he endured some serious pain, including the realization that the wives of himself and his soldiers had been taken captive by the enemy. (See 1 Samuel 30:1–3.) Such experiences ultimately grew the faith of Joseph and David, but in the moment, these men endured intense pain—and intense confusion over why God would subject them to it.

Joseph had to do the work of a slave, bear the pain of a reputation ruined by false allegations, and subsist on prison food. I'm fairly sure there were hundreds of times he wished he had never talked about those dreams of his! *I wish I hadn't opened my big mouth*, he probably thought. *I wish I hadn't trusted my brothers. Why did I do that? What an idiot I am! How could I be so stupid?*

David felt the betrayal of his friends who wanted him dead. They were pals for life when he was "slaying his tens of thousands" (see 1 Samuel 18:7). They were down to ride. But when they lost their families and felt David was to blame, they started looking for rocks.

"Yes, brother, but that was God's 'training for reigning' for Joseph and David," you may tell me. Sure. Easy for us to say as we quip our prefabbed, churchy slogans.

It was not so easy for Joseph and David. They had to endure it, feel it, go through it. They were probably plagued with the "what ifs," second-guessing their beliefs and the people they had chosen to trust. These two men—a once-favored son and a once-famous giant killer—found themselves in the gutter, feeling that life wasn't worth living. They may even, like George Bailey in the movie *It's a Wonderful Life*, have wished they had never been born. It's hard to stay focused on the big picture when everything in your life is crumbling. It's so much easier to run away.

Turning to drugs, sexual sin, perversion, gluttony, and drunkenness might seem attractive for the moment. It would have been easy for the minister to tell the doctor, "Put that needle away. You know, my boy doesn't need a shot." There are several famous preachers today who preach that Jesus didn't need to go to the cross, and it's easy for their hearers to find logic in their statements and believe this falsehood. It's easy for them to preach a half gospel that sounds good, and people buy their books, talk about what great leaders they are, and comment on how "enlightened" they've become. Watering down the message of the gospel to remove "offensive" truths like hell, the need for Jesus to suffer and die for our sins, and our need to give up our sinful behavior in response may be popular and easy to follow, but it leads to death. Having ice cream and cotton candy is fun for the moment, but it kills in the long run, just like sin.

Unfortunately for our comfort-craving flesh, the easy way is not the right way. The best way to bear fruit for the kingdom of God is not done by taking the easy road or the pleasant, pansied path.

The minister who had to hold his son down during a booster shot was willing to let his boy experience physical pain and the emotional pain of perceived betrayal because it was the best thing for him. God allowed Joseph to be taken from his family, stripped of his multicolored coat and his dignity, betrayed by his brothers, and purchased as a slave. "Why would a 'loving' God do that?" one could understandably ask. The simple answer is that suffering is part of the gospel. When we suffer, we identify with Jesus and with other people who are hurting. When we suffer, we remember what is important, and it brings clarity to our priorities. When we suffer, we are reminded of our temporary station here on earth and the fragility of our existence. When we suffer for the kingdom's sake, we craft for ourselves crowns of honor that we can lay at our Savior's feet. Love, true love, is tested in obedience and suffering. Jesus was tested, and likewise those who follow Him will be tested.

True grace is transformational by nature. It doesn't leave the drunkard drunk; it doesn't abandon the addict to his addiction. True grace lifts us out of the gutter. It teaches us responsibility; it causes us to grow up. It transforms us from the inside out. This process takes time, and our flesh is sure to fight back. But if we don't compromise the message, heaven will come and help us. True grace, not greasy grace, must win the day. Now is the time to swap the cheap, false hope of greasy grace for the transformational truth and freedom found in true grace.

4

IDENTIFYING THE FAKE ROLEX OF THEOLOGY

While traveling overseas, I have seen vendors selling counterfeit watches that are imitations of a well-known brand name. Casual observers can't tell the difference between a genuine Rolex watch and a fake, and many are content to settle for the counterfeit, as long as it looks like the real thing and keeps time. To its credit, a counterfeit Rolex is definitely affordable, and you don't feel as bad if it breaks. However, this status symbol that seems to represent luxury ultimately has very little true value.

The greasy-grace gospel is the fake Rolex of theology. The indifferent don't care. They want something that looks enough like the real thing without the price. I liken it to a preacher who pushes people over at the altar, making it look like they got "hit" by the Holy Spirit's power. To get a real anointing is costly, and, while some people are so overwhelmed by God's power when they are prayed for that they fall over, falsely duplicating the experience doesn't benefit the seekers who haven't yet found what they were looking for.

The costly kind of anointing takes hours of prayer, worship, obedience, fasting, sacrifice, denial of self, and a sensitivity to the Spirit that only comes from brokenness. It's so much "cheaper" and easier to gently push people over, fabricating their "being slain in the Spirit," than to pay the price of having God's manifest presence in your life and in your church. No one I ever met with a nickel's worth of anointing came by it quickly and easily. Among those truly anointed, suffering has consistently been their portion.

But when someone goes through death and resurrection to get something genuine from God, results are guaranteed. When there are miracles, signs, and wonders, and when power is tangibly felt, it brings blessing and, in many cases, immediate or eventual notoriety, honor, book sales, invitations, prosperity, and so forth. Many ministers want all these things but aren't willing to die to self, labor in prayer, or lay down their lives for the sake of God's kingdom. They learn that the "fake Rolex" anointing is much less costly than the genuine article, so they manufacture the outward signs that make it appear as if they have the real presence of God in their lives. If they pull this off effectively, they will receive the privileges of God's anointed servants. It is a "fake Rolex" anointing, and the cost is attractive to those who aren't prepared to pay the high price of true discipleship.

This is one result of greasy grace—an unwillingness to give the appropriate response to the true grace lavished so freely on us. It's a shortcut, so to speak, that combines humanistic philosophy, twisted Scriptures, and manipulation of those who lack understanding, creating the fake Rolex of Christianity. Instead of going through the process, they make statements that show themselves to be self-assured and convince the undiscerning that they have had a so-called special revelation, telling such believers, for example, "If you could only understand God's real grace, then you could live a life as free and unburdened as mine." Anyone who contradicts their stance, they label as "religious," "self-righteous," "old-fashioned," or "stuck in the past."

THE "ENLIGHTENED" FAÇADE
OF GREASY-GRACE PREACHERS

The cheap-grace camp operators use sleight of hand, with the same appearance of doing good while doing something sinister. Masquerading as one who wants to be "loving" or "gracious," those in the "sloppy agape" crowd operate with sinister motivations, not the least of which is the desire to be liked by their listeners.

Greasy-grace preachers love accolades. The opinion of others is paramount to them. They crack another proverbial beer bottle of cheap liquid grace for the person engrossed in sin to slurp up, not because they love them but because they themselves want to be loved, revered, or seen as "enlightened." They peddle a Christianity that "sells" by being inclusive and relevant.

They don't want to be lumped in with Bible-thumping "funda-mentalists" who are "mean" or "out of touch." They want to be seen not as "religious" but rather as "spiritual."

The truth is, none of us wants to be associated with mean, angry people. We all want to be heard, and a lot of us want to be liked or even loved by the public. Regardless, when a public opinion or fashionable thought pollutes the gospel mes-sage, waters down the teaching of the Scriptures, and compro-mises our faithfulness to the truth, we have ceased being true preachers of the gospel and have turned into sock puppets and politicians.

In such a realm of falsities, we may appear to be loving those we lead, but we are really enabling them in self-destruc-tive beliefs and behaviors, both on earth and for eternity. We are sending them down the wide road that leads to destruction. And we're doing it for ourselves, to save face and preserve our popularity.

WE MAY APPEAR TO BE LOVING
THOSE WE LEAD, BUT IT COULD BE THAT WE
ARE REALLY ENABLING THEM IN
SELF-DESTRUCTIVE BELIEFS AND BEHAVIORS,
ON EARTH AND FOR ETERNITY.

Walking in the truth of Scripture is often countercultural. There is an inherent conflict that arises when you walk with Jesus, believing, acting, and doing what He said. Nobody wants the insults, the accusations, or the threats. We don't want to be defamed by the media. We want to give our children another ice cream cone, another cotton candy; we want to stuff their purses and wallets full of tens and twenties. Just like Peter did, we want to tell Jesus not to go to the cross. "Life is good, Jesus; let's leave out all that stuff about dying." We give people a gospel that costs them nothing.

THAT WHICH COSTS ME NOTHING

Life can be a primrose path for preachers who omit the entire message of the cross. They go on popular talk shows, getting promoted by the media, while embracing a perversion that God's word calls an abomination. They get the favor of man— and lose the favor of God.

They sell lots of books to fellow snowflakes who have not learned, as my grandfather did growing up on a Texas farm and sacrificing for his country overseas, that suffering can be one of life's greatest teachers. They have not learned that indulging in sin while invoking God's grace is not loving the Lord or people.

In fact, it is quite the opposite. We need to love. To do so, we have to learn what love actually means.

Champions of the greasy-grace gospel feel that love equates with permissiveness. They think that love is a participation medal with extra pampering and doting, to boot. But that isn't love. It's a perversion that enables people to continue down a feel-good path that ends in an excruciating eternity.

Greasy-grace preachers want all the benefits of Jesus's sacrifice with none of the cost it demands of them. But that is not how the kingdom of God works. In 2 Samuel 24, we see King David demonstrating how to operate with God's kingdom principles in mind.

DAVID SHOWS THE WAY

David had messed up in a big way. Whatever David did, he did it in a big way. If he did something right, he went all out, but the same was true when he did something wrong. In this chapter, he did something wrong in a big, hulking way.

God had brought David up from nothing. He started out as a nobody, a lowly shepherd boy who didn't earn much respect. His own family didn't show much affection for him and, in some cases, could only ridicule him. From that humble position, God blessed him beyond his wildest imagination, eventually making him king.

Not only did He make him king, but He made him a successful king by uniting Judah and Israel. Because God brought David from low places to sit on the throne, David had every reason to put his hope in God and not trust in himself. Trusting in himself, at this point, would have been an outright insult to God. God was the one who had brought him up from nothing, and he owed God the courtesy of trust.

Unfortunately, as is common among many heroes, he blew it. He told his general to count the number of his soldiers. On the surface, it seemed like a reasonable request. What military leader wouldn't want to know how many soldiers he had? What was the harm in it? But when we consider the matter more closely in context, we see that David was insulting the Lord by issuing this command. He was "trusting in chariots" (see Psalm 20:7) instead of trusting God.

The Lord was incensed, and judgment fell swiftly on David and those under his leadership. The punishment was gruesome, and he couldn't wait for it to stop. When it ended, the prophet

Gad told David to make an altar and sacrifice to the Lord on the threshing floor of Araunah the Jebusite. (See 2 Samuel 24:18–25.)

As David approached, Araunah asked David what he was doing there. David said he wanted to buy his threshing floor and oxen so he could sacrifice to the Lord. We are unclear about Araunah's motives. Maybe he was fearful, perhaps he felt respect, or maybe he was shaken by God's judgment, as well, and wanted to participate in the offering. Whatever the reason, he wanted to give David the threshing floor and oxen for free. So, he said, "Take it; it's yours." (See 2 Samuel 24:22–23.) Then and there, David showed why he was a man after God's own heart.

Yes, David sinned a lot; yes, he'd just made a fresh, huge mistake that cost 70,000 lives. Yet he was still a man after God's own heart. David understood the ways of the Lord. He understood the importance of one's heart attitude, and his subsequent actions constituted sincere repentance that shifted the troubling situation. After being offered free oxen and a threshing floor, David, in poignant words, said, "I will not give to the Lord that which costs me nothing" (see 2 Samuel 24:24).

THE APOSTLE PAUL ECHOES DAVID

A prevailing sentiment of the greasy-grace gospel is that relaxation and enjoyment are paramount. Anything difficult or unpleasant needs to be removed. Such discomforts as fasting, abstinence, and self-denial are maligned as "religious," Old Covenant "works" by those who advance such pursuits as kicking back, soaking up the sun, and enjoying God's grace bought by Jesus's death. After all, that's why Jesus died, right? So we can be comfortable at all costs?

It is precisely what happens when you relate to God through philosophical means instead of a real relationship. People who prize intellect often struggle to move past a conceptual relationship with God to a heart-connected one. A real relationship with the Lord pushes you out to the edge of faith and sacrifice. Comfort comes by the true and lavish grace of the Lord, but that comfort comes in the middle of the battle, not in avoiding it. God's genuine grace is an empowering presence that enables us to thrive amid difficult times, and it is only in those times that we begin to understand the extent of that grace.

The apostle Paul taught more about God's empowering grace than most preachers do today. Paul experienced and preached a grace to suffer, work hard, and give your very life for Christ—not a cheap imitation of grace that encourages people to sit back, relax, and trust in God's promises.

Here is Paul's story:

I have worked much harder than anyone, been in prison more frequently than anyone, been flogged more severely than anyone, and been exposed to death again and again. Five times I received from the Jews the forty lashes minus one. Three times I was beaten with rods, once I was pelted with stones, three times I was shipwrecked; I spent a night and a day in the open sea; I have been constantly on the move. I have been in danger from rivers, in danger from bandits, in danger from my fellow Jews, in danger from Gentiles; in danger in the city, in danger in the country, in danger at sea, and in danger from false believers. I have labored and toiled and have often gone without sleep; I have known hunger and thirst and have often gone without food; I have been cold and naked. Besides everything else, I face daily the pressure of my concern for all the churches. Who is weak, and I do not feel weak? Who is led into sin, and I do not inwardly burn? If I must boast, I will boast of the things that show my weakness.   (2 Corinthians 11:23–30)

Paul wasn't looking to use Jesus's blood as an excuse for self-indulgence. He wasn't looking to philosophize his way out of a struggle so he could reach a place of comfort and relaxation. Instead, he willingly endured discomfort, pain, and toil, having learned in all circumstances to be content because of the grace of God. (See Philippians 4:11–13.)

As he continued writing, Paul described an "angel" or messenger from Satan, what he called a *"thorn in the flesh"* (2 Corinthians 12:7). We don't know the exact nature of his "thorn," but we know that it was tormenting Paul. It was so bad that after being tortured, left for dead, and shipwrecked, Paul pleaded with God to take it away. It must have been horrible.

After the third time Paul begged God to take away the thorn, what was God's answer? "You need more relaxation"? No! After begging God, in the middle of his suffering, Paul received this answer. *"He said to me, 'My grace is sufficient for you, for my power is made perfect in weakness'"* (2 Corinthians 12:9).

GRACE TO OVERCOME

While greasy grace wants relaxation, God wants us to be empowered by His grace to suffer many things, and, yes, to overcome those things. Helen Keller once said, "Although the world is full of great suffering, it is also full of the overcoming of it."[7] God's grace is free, but it isn't cheap.

Instead of preaching about the kind of sacrifice Paul endured by the empowerment of grace, many Christian leaders emphasize the act of resting and relaxing in the promises of God. Something tells me that Paul, while being pummeled with rocks, facing starvation, or suffering from the thorn in the flesh, wasn't "resting and relaxing." On the contrary, he was in pain, begging God for help. However, he was also trusting in authentic, costly grace—not cheap, greasy grace—to see him through. As Paul described in his letters, real grace gives us the power to have victory even in the worst suffering, at our weakest, because we are overcomers.

REAL GRACE GIVES US THE POWER
TO HAVE VICTORY EVEN IN THE WORST
SUFFERING, AT OUR WEAKEST,
BECAUSE WE ARE OVERCOMERS.

The greasy-grace gospel omits talk of sacrifice and cost. There's no emphasis on picking up one's cross and following Jesus, because "Jesus paid it all." Those who subscribe to this false gospel take the free oxen and threshing floor and give the Lord a "sacrifice" of conveniences and ease instead of seeking to live out the words and teachings of the One who died for us so that we might all have the courage to die the death to which we are called.

---

7. https://www.brainyquote.com/quotes/helen_keller_109208.

Now is the time for the church to rise up and say, with David, "Jesus paid such a price that I will not make my life a living sacrifice that costs me nothing. I will drink from the cup that Jesus gives me to drink." But our culture shouts the opposite sentiment, as we will see in the next chapter.

5

THE SPREAD OF
THE SNOWFLAKE GOSPEL

True Grace leads to Godly life,
a life that seeks after God. A life where our joy and
delight are to follow and serve Jesus.
—Ibrahim Emile[8]

In 2016, *Collins English Dictionary* added the term "snowflake generation" to its annals, defined as "the young adults of the 2010s, viewed as being less resilient and more prone to taking offence than previous generations."[9] Let me say that when I use

---

8. GoodReads.com, https://www.goodreads.com/author/quotes/8728717. Ibrahim_Emile.
9. "Top 10 Collins Words of the Year 2016," Collins language lovers blog, https://blog.collinsdictionary.com/language-lovers/top-10-collins-words-of-the-year-2016/.

the term "snowflakes," I am not talking about millennials, specifically and exclusively. I have encountered many thoughtful, remarkable millennials with uncompromising courage, a willingness to die to the flesh, and a desire to engage in self-sacrifice. Many millennials, believers and nonbelievers alike, demonstrate integrity and a sincere desire to do what is right.

We can all agree while every generation has its snowflakes, this demographic is well-represented among millennials. They're known for being weak-willed excuse-makers with an acquired victim mentality who avoid suffering at all costs and advocate participation trophies for all. Characteristically, they don't run toward the battle; they run away from it. That's because they don't understand the potential value of suffering, discipline, and self-denial. Many snowflakes were raised without positive role models, especially male ones; it is common for them to have been coddled and babied by their mothers. Once grown up, they pamper themselves and devote themselves to the fulfillment of their creature comforts.

A "GOSPEL" TAILOR-MADE FOR TODAY'S SNOWFLAKES

"Christian snowflakes" often know more about essential oils than the essential truths of Scripture. They run at the first sign of trouble, whine when difficulties appear, and could be classified, from a character perspective, as spineless. Political correctness and "wokeness" are their primary goals, and they follow the crowd, seeking safety in numbers. The protection they seek is the same protection that previous generations lived without. In the face of disagreements, they pursue "safe spaces," avoiding conflict at all costs. On the public streets, they shriek dramatically when their favorite presidential candidate isn't elected.

Once-respected universities now serve as grown baby coddling stations where "therapeutic" coloring books and cocoa stations placate and pamper these adult infants.

While my grandfather studied by day and worked by night through his college years to help his family back on the farm, modern-day snowflakes argue that their student loans should be wiped away because, after all, they are "special." The snowflake subculture has birthed such societal phenomena as gender confusion, cancel culture, and a cultural model of "guilty even if proven innocent" when the accusation is something along the lines of sexual misconduct or racism. Too often, when women accuse men for any reason, there is no due process. Calling someone racist has become a manipulative tool to bypass a dialogue sharing both points of view. Snowflakes look to the government to provide for and protect them, demanding compensation for their own lack of responsibility from the cradle to the grave. With the loss of a significant male role model contributing to their lives and upbringing, many have lost their way, and most, if not all, have lost their moral compass, as well.

When my grandfather was in his early twenties, he was fighting the Battle of the Bulge, taking ground from the Nazis, and watching friends die on either side of him. He and so many other young men sacrificed their lives, while the young women back home were sacrificing care of their families to work in a factory or supporting the fight for freedom in other ways. Snowflakes, on the other hand, find their passion for promoting perverted causes that have been well-established as mental illnesses and seem to live in a state of continual outrage against sensible things.

Typically, they won't sacrifice their lives for others in literal battles, such as those my grandfather faced, but they will work to champion ungodly sexual acts, drug use, and the spewing of hate-filled speech to anyone who would dare to disagree with them. After all, anyone who disagrees with you must have some kind of "phobia."

"Do what you want. You only live once!" "Smoke what you wish and have sex with whomever or whatever you want to." "Your gender is how you feel." These statements reflect the cultural atmosphere today, when spiritualism is in, but religious faith is out. Feelings, not facts, reign supreme in their tiny world, where logic is confronted on every side and treated with disdain. Being nice has far eclipsed being honest in terms of importance.

Can you see why the greasy-grace gospel appeals to snowflakes? They want a form of love that doesn't require anything of them. They want the benefits of faith without the prescribed disciplines, duties, and responsibilities that go along with it. The greasy-grace gospel is a custom-tailored doctrine for people who want to be able to do nothing while feeling entitled to everything. Greasy-grace theology and snowflake ideology are a match made in hell—a hell whose existence many Christian snowflakes would deny.

The concepts of entitlement, privilege, and participation trophies that are earned just for showing up are totally in sync with the "feel-good" gospel of greasy grace, where feelings are the highest priority. Truth, discipline, devotion, and duty—all required and reasonable responses to true grace—are viewed with the skeptical stink eye of greasy grace.

"That's religion!" they shout as they sit on cushy church chairs, wanting to hear just one more message about how much

God loves them. They want to sing one more song about how special they are to God, but with no mention of the cross, no talk of dying to the flesh, no notions of commitment, devotion, or duty. To them, those things aren't fun, nor do they feel good. Greasy grace goes down easy, and snowflakes love it.

GOD'S LOVE AND ITS REQUIREMENTS—WHAT THE SNOWFLAKE GOSPEL FORGOT

The most significant expression of God's love to us is this: *"While we were still sinners, Christ died for us"* (Romans 5:8). We were still stuck on the fool's path when God loved us so much that He sent us His Son. Jesus died for us while we were still in our sins. This is grace—true grace, lavish grace.

With true grace, God extends an underserved hand to the foolish, blind, and wicked. Some people think that original sin doesn't exist. Some feel that humanity is "pretty good" overall. This is nonsense.

If you doubt that humans are inherently wicked, go to a theater of war and see what humans do when lifting societal restraints observed in times of peace. Or research what happens when leaders with unchecked power deal with those who would dare to challenge them. Or simply put two toddlers in a playpen with a single toy and watch what happens. In all likelihood, you won't witness peace, love, and harmony. "Mine!" is the cry of the wicked human heart. Humans are depraved. We are full of sin from our beginning and in desperate need of a Savior. So, a Hand outstretched from a flawless God toward dark, depraved humanity is true and lavish grace, and it's a necessary step for any real heart transformation to take place within us.

Such grace is the most generous gift that has ever been given. Still, the Hand must be received. The seed can fall to the ground, but the ground must open up so that the dirt receives it. Humanity must open itself and respond to receive. Certainly, the ground gives nutrients to the seed, but the seed is the greater gift, and both remain fruitless without each other's contribution.

Greasy-grace fanboys will tell you there's nothing you have to do, because no one can add to what God has done. Yet you have to open your heart and contribute what you have—all you have—or you can't receive God's grace. Your spiritual growth, in response to receiving grace, is proof that you have received a work of grace. When soil and seed mix, a transformation takes place. Growth happens. Fruitfulness occurs. However, both must be willing participants. Without one or the other, they both remain as they are. The dirt is not adding to the seed but receiving the seed, after which point it has an ongoing partnership with the seed to produce fruit.

If the seed begged the dirt for its simple daily contribution, it would enable the soil in its dysfunctionality. Someone might defend the soil, saying, "The soil has a good heart; it's just not ready to give of its nutrients." Or, "The seed is all you need, but who do you think you are, dirt, that you could add one thing to what the seed has done?" Without question, the dirt makes only a modest contribution, but it does everything in its power. A widow's mite wasn't an impressive amount, monetarily speaking, but the effort to contribute all she had showed the sincerity of her heart. (See, for example, Luke 21:1–4.)

Questions spoken in a tone of accusation are the modus operandi of many greasy-grace preachers. "Who do you think you are, trying to 'strive'? Jesus finished the work on the cross!"

"I cannot add one thing to what Jesus has done; my actions are meaningless, for it's all about Jesus." Half-truths always sound enticing, and they are the manipulation required to promote a doctrine that is clearly not biblical.

HALF-TRUTHS ARE THE MANIPULATION REQUIRED TO PROMOTE A DOCTRINE THAT IS CLEARLY NOT BIBLICAL.

Euphemistically speaking, greasy grace is the enabling wife buying another six pack for her unemployed, abusive drunkard of a husband at home. It's the pastor who, in counseling sessions with lost church member who are walking in perversion, gleefully pats them on the back and assures them, "You were born this way. God made you like this! Enjoy!"

It's the mother at the Texas fair wanting to compensate for her deprived childhood by spoiling her son beyond what is healthy for him. It's the peasant-farmer-turned-educated-war-hero-turned-citywide-leader who never had two fives to rub together as a youth and wants "more" for his daughter, whose well-intended efforts to better her upbringing inadvertently cripple her financially for a lifetime. Greasy grace is the easy way out, the cross-less Christianity, the fake Rolex watch of theology.

RELIGION—WHERE ALL THINGS GO WRONG

In my thirties, my first marriage had just ended, the worldwide revival movement I was a part of imploded, and I threw in the towel. How did I do this? By taking a speedy nosedive into sin. I went back to my old habits. (Actually, my old habits probably blushed at my new approach.) I didn't care anymore. I didn't care about other people's opinions, nor did I care about my ministry, future, or reputation. I was almost hoping I would be found out and exposed so I would never have to deal with "all that church stuff" again.

In the church, we have "acceptable" sins like gluttony, gossip, uncontrollable tempers…all the stuff that is safe to mention, the stuff that makes us look "honest" and "real." Even though these things may be called out in sermons, few people do anything to address these issues or make changes in their lives. "My pastor tells it like it is," you protest. The truth is, in many cases, your pastor tells you only what you will accept without leaving his church. We ministry leaders have a nose for what are "acceptable" sins and what are not. If the truth were laid bare, you would likely make a quick exit and never come back.

"Church sins" are behaviors and actions that are okay with man, even if they aren't okay with God. Sexual sins, on the other hand, are not "acceptable" church sins; in many conservative religious circles, they are the unforgivable sin that results in "disqualification" from grace.

The Western fascination and obsession with sexual sins traces back to our nation's Puritan roots. In an attempt to be holy and set apart, the Puritans went overboard, effectively demonizing sexuality and sexual desires, never mind their God-given nature in the context of marriage. This approach made it a recognized sin in church circles to enjoy sex, even by married couples. Sexual acts were permitted solely for the purpose of procreation, nothing more; sexual pleasure fell under the devil's domain.

In the Plymouth Colony, they more or less followed the Levitical law. Sexual sin was against secular law at the time, and those found guilty of it were publicly whipped for fornication. Adultery was punished by publicly whipping; in some cases, the guilty party was branded with a hot iron and forced to wear a sewn letter "A" (for convicted adultery) on their clothing. The same steps were followed for a rapist, only with the letter "R." Rape, "buggery" (sex with animals), and "sodomy" (men having sex with men) were all punishable by death.[10]

While we must remain pure, holy, and sexually clean, man's attempts to get there without the work of the Holy Spirit created religion and rules in place of true sanctification. The aftereffect in our culture has been disastrous. Among the eventualities of sexual deviance are abortion, child sexual molestation, and the record-breaking creation and distribution of pornographic material. Why? Because puritanical man-made religion didn't understand that purity comes by change from the inside out. Purity is a result of a real relationship with God. You become pure by being around purity, meaning the One who is pure. You must spend time with the Lord to gain holiness, not simply follow the rules because you fear punishment.

Transformation, sanctification, and cleansing can only come from a genuine relationship with the Lord. Sometimes, it takes time. Some people are transformed more quickly or by a different process from others. However, followers of manufactured religion don't see it that way; they always wash the outside of the cup. (See Matthew 23:25.) Religion cares about embarrassment, shame, the opinions of men, and how things "look."

---

10. Lisa M. Lauria, "Sexual Misconduct in Plymouth Colony," The Plymouth Colony Archive Project, 1998, copyright Patricia Scott Deetz and Christopher Fennell, http://www.histarch.illinois.edu/plymouth/Lauria1.html.

With stones in hand, religion is always ready to kill the woman caught in adultery. (See John 8:1–11.) I always thought it curious that the woman alone was caught. Was she slower than the man? Likely, she was just easier to apprehend. In the stone-throwers' gallant attempt to uphold the religious standard, they invariably attacked the weak and vulnerable. When someone has a weakness or a vulnerability, "Churchianity"—man-made religion, Pharisaism—is always ready to start throwing stones.

> TRANSFORMATION, SANCTIFICATION, AND CLEANSING CAN ONLY COME FROM A GENUINE RELATIONSHIP WITH THE LORD.

And Jesus is the one who stands in defense of these weak ones, these sinners, these ones caught in sin. He quickly points out to those who would throw stones that their sins, though "acceptable" in church, are not acceptable to God. They throw stones with dirty hands.

TRANSFORMATIVE, CONFRONTATIONAL GRACE VERSUS CHEAP, FAKE GRACE

However, sin is sin. It's a condition resulting in judgment and punishment. As I mentioned, when I was in my thirties, I engaged in serious sin. Ungodliness. And several years later, the Lord revealed to me my bitterness toward Him for the life circumstances that led me astray. When you feel bitter, sin is often your refuge because that bitterness blocks your communion with God.

I didn't commit "church sins"; I committed the sins that anger the Pharisees, Puritans, and stone-throwers. It wasn't gluttony or gossip or "anger issues"; on the contrary, it was "real" sin that I was involved with for several years.

I share this regrettable part of my journey in order to emphasize that I didn't need cheap, fake, greasy grace. A few platitudes about the "finished work" of Jesus Christ wouldn't get me free. I didn't need people to tell me the sin I was involved with was okay, or that what I was doing wasn't a sin. I was missing the mark, with consequences for myself and, more important, for those I loved. I needed a truth encounter. I needed real grace, confrontational grace—grace that didn't excuse me but rather would transform me.

The way out wasn't a bumper-sticker slogan of cheap grace that reads, "Jesus loves you just the way you are"; "Jesus paid it all, so don't worry"; "You can't add anything to your salvation"; "You are striving if you try to change. Remember, it's not about 'works.'"

I wasn't striving; I was sinning, and I knew better. When I received the baptism of the Holy Spirit, the Lord delivered me of three demons, and I saw them come out. He did a cleansing, reparative work so deep that, for many years after, there was a guard for purity on my mind and spirit such that sin was repulsive to me.

This happened not because I was "trying" but because it was an outcome of true grace and real relationship, a transformation from the inside out. It was not a pharisaical outward cleansing of the cup for appearance's sake but a genuine, deep work of God. I knew what was right and wrong, and I knew what sin was and what wasn't. I knew my problem wasn't just a failure to understand how big God's grace is or any other cheesy, feel-good slogan. I was in sin.

I genuinely tried. I fasted, prayed, and did all the other things, but until the Lord showed me that I was bitter and needed to forgive, I could not get free. After the Lord showed me my bitterness, I was able to repent and get free. Thankfully, by God's grace, I have been free in this area for years.

After I embraced that move of true, confrontational grace, God started moving in my life. It was a movement of true grace, but it was also God's extravagant mercy. That's why I talk about it so often—because true grace is what we all desperately need. True grace showed me that the key to my freedom was letting go of bitterness, and it was true grace that restored my life. True grace brought me and my wife, Kate, to a healthy, godly relationship. True grace gave me the ability to overcome the snare of those sins that had gotten me off track so easily.

TRUE GRACE SHOWED ME THAT THE KEY TO MY FREEDOM WAS LETTING GO OF BITTERNESS. IT WAS TRUE GRACE THAT RESTORED MY LIFE.

THE IMPOTENCE OF FAKE GRACE

This is why I hate fake grace so much. It doesn't set the captive free; it pats the captive on the back, reassuring him as he plods along his road to destruction. Fake, cheap, greasy grace doesn't transform. Greasy grace leaves those ensnared in sin stuck while heaps of feel-good words pile on them. Externally, it feels good—have your sin and eat it, too—but, deep down, there is no peace because we have not stepped into the freedom God has offered us.

Fake grace is the enemy of true grace because it pretends to be something it's not. It doesn't empower or set free, but it sweeps things under the rug with slogans and philosophy. The head might like the reasoning, but the heart knows it's wrong. Those with discernment can see the difference.

Jesus didn't rail against the tax-collecting crooks or the prostitutes, but He unleashed his anger at the Pharisees because they pretended to offer a solution through rules and manufactured philosophies that God alone could provide through the work of His Holy Spirit. The greasy-grace approach claims to represent God without actually knowing Him.

The Pharisees were counterfeit; Jesus was the real deal. The same is true with greasy grace, the counterfeit to authentic religion. It's a false hope, an insincere promise, and a twisted perspective. It's fake, but people in sin need the "real deal." I needed the real thing when I was stuck in darkness. Hollow reassurances and shallow words couldn't help. I needed true grace, a grace that truthfully shifts things in our lives. True grace, lavish grace, doesn't tell someone they are okay when they aren't; it empowers them to overcome their sin and get free, truly free.

A WORD TO MILLENNIALS

I have a heart for millennials. They have been sold the cheap-grace lie and are stuck. They have a gospel that requires no sacrifice, no commitment, and no "overcoming." "Jesus paid it all" is a truth that has been used in a deceptive way. Jesus *did* pay it all...so that we would "go and do likewise," meaning we must give *our* all, as well.

Just yesterday, I saw an honest social media post I found disturbing. This young man's transparency was only matched by his depth of bondage. His post said, in effect, "I just don't get it. I have been told Christ has done it all for me, that I am already transformed, that I have become like Christ. Yet I watch hours of porn and smoke loads of weed every day. When is this grace thing supposed to kick in? I want to be like Jesus, I've been told it's already been done, but it ain't working for me."

When I read his expletive-laced post, I became angry at the way the false gospel being preached today has imposed shackles of confusion on people who want to walk with Christ. The lie has made such an inroad that the truth almost seems to be a rare example. The millennial, pampered by his parents, now lives in their basement because they crippled him with "love." The millennial pampered by their pastor lives in the spiritual basement. And neither one understands what is wrong, why they are lost. It's completely demonic.

True grace is completely different. True grace is the father that says to his adult child, "You have one month to get out of the basement. I love you, but it's time to grow up and be an adult." The father pats the child on the back as they leave, and the mother cries, but they both know it's best for their child. A father's love majors on the combination of truth and love. A father understands that either one without the other is imbalanced.

Our heavenly Father also demonstrates this kind of love. Hebrews 11:6 says, "*The Lord disciplines the one he loves, and he chastens everyone he accepts as his son."* According to the gospel of Christ, you must die to live, you must be last to be first, and you must suffer many things for the gospel. As the apostle Paul wrote, we must share in Christ's suffering, just as we share in His glory. (See Romans 8:17.) True grace empowers us to embrace the suffering that leads to the glory we all hope for and desire. The message of this book is for everyone who has been duped by the lie of cheap grace, but particularly the millennials, many of whom have been fed this feel-good lie their whole life and whom God is now calling forward out of the false and into the real.

6

THE PENDULUM'S SWING

Someone once asked me how the church had gotten suckered into the false teaching of cheap grace. I told him I believed it was a reflection of our culture and a lack of scriptural knowledge. As a caveat, culture has its merits. It is sometimes through the lens of culture that we see God in a new way or perceive a truth of Scripture in a new light. Culture can be a contributing factor to our spiritual growth. However, if we don't genuinely press into an ever-deepening walk with God, our surrounding culture will likely diminish and even start to dominate our theological understanding. It is through a cultural lens that we view life, church, God, friends, family, and more. This is unavoidable. We all do it. But if we really seek to know the Lord, we are empowered and enlightened to see our culture through biblically informed eyes, so that we are not taken in or deceived by it. The alternative is our surrounding culture rising up and coloring our theological viewpoints and scriptural interpretations, making us conform more and more to the world with merely a Christian veneer.

IF WE REALLY SEEK TO KNOW THE LORD, WE ARE EMPOWERED AND ENLIGHTENED TO SEE OUR CULTURE THROUGH BIBLICALLY INFORMED EYES, SO THAT WE ARE NOT TAKEN IN OR DECEIVED BY IT.

One of two things happens in the church: either the church stands against ungodly social norms, or ungodly social norms influence the church. Scripture is the only accurate measuring rod. When we know what God's Word truly says, we are not easily fooled. But when we negate our pursuit of biblical knowledge, then the flesh takes over, and our evil desires begin to creep in. Unchecked by the Word of God, those desires seal our doom.

Yet, thanks to God for His true grace, there is hope in our Redeemer. I believe the Lord would say to the believer whose ears have been tickled by the gospel of cheap grace, "Reject the greasy-grace gospel. Come to true grace, lavish grace, a grace that transforms, not condones or enables. If your father wasn't around or wasn't interested, allow Me to be your Father. Someone must teach you right from wrong, truth from lies, reality from falsehood. Life with Me won't always be easy, and you will be challenged by the hard truths. But if you can accept the true message of grace, your life will be rewarding, deeply satisfying, and important; and, in the end, you will reap a reward for what you have done and spend eternity with the redeemed."

THE POLAR OPPOSITE OF FAKE GRACE... AND HOW IT PROMPTED AN "ANYTHING GOES" THEOLOGY

That message would have been helpful to members of the movement that paved the way for cheap grace as a reactionary route to the works-based piety the Pentecostal faith is known for. Statistically, Pentecostalism and the Neo-Pentecostal movement constitute the largest voluntary sociological people movement in the history of the world. According to the *World Christian Encyclopedia*, over 8 percent of the world's population—644 million people—are Pentecostal or Neo-Pentecostal (the term "Charismatic" encompassing both).[11] This group includes all people who can trace their spiritual roots back to the Azusa Street Revival in the early 1900s in Los Angeles, California.

Of course, numerically, those practicing Islam and Catholicism constitute larger groups than Pentecostals. But when you consider that much of the growth of those two religions was forced or coerced conversion, you cannot classify them as "voluntary" sociological movements. Catholicism and Islam are both largely "movements of the sword," meaning they

---

11. Todd M. Johnson and Gina A. Zurlo, *World Christian Encyclopedia*, 3rd ed. (Edinburgh: Edinburgh University Press, 2020), 5, quoted in Nimi Wariboko and L. William Oliverio Jr., "The Society for Pentecostal Studies at 50 Years: Ways Forward for Pentecostalism," *Pneuma*, Brill online, December 9, 2020, https://brill.com/view/journals/pneu/42/3-4/article-p327_1.xml?language=en#:~:text=In%20terms%20of%20overall%20numbers,affiliation%20is%20with%20other%20churches.

employ, or historically have employed, a convert-or-die tactic to win converts and expand. Catholicism does not do this any longer, but there are parts of the world today where their influence is due to a wielding of the sword centuries ago. Both groups also have built-in theological procreation theologies that ensure their continued growth, with large families of children who did not convert to the faith based on a personal encounter with "truth" or from a deeply spiritual experience but simply because they were born to a practicing family

Pentecostalism and Neo-Pentecostalism, on the other hand, grew strictly by way of personal conversion, from the heartfelt convictions of individuals who believed in what they were hearing and experiencing. These individuals weren't added to the institution's rolls by the sword or through birth but by an experience and conviction that God is present and active in their lives—by simple, heartfelt conviction.

PENTECOSTAL HOLINESS—
HUMBLE BEGINNINGS WITH WIDESPREAD INFLUENCE

What started as a simple home prayer meeting on Bonnie Brae Street in Los Angeles, California, just seven and a half miles from where I was writing this, would go on to shake up the world. It all happened in a period of just over a hundred years. For now, we see only a glimpse of the impact on culture, history, and our views on morality. The centuries to come will document just how impactful their contribution will be.

Pentecostals originally came from what is known as the Holiness tradition, which emphasized pleasing God by excising from one's life anything that was not acceptable to the Lord. The Holiness group had a tremendously intense focus on what they called "personal holiness," with sexual purity, right motives about money, avoiding worldly entertainment, modest dress, clean speech, and commitment to daily prayer and devotion at the forefront.

Those in the Holiness movement made a conscious, consistent, and persistent effort to "clean up their life." In spite of their acknowledgment that human effort alone wouldn't suffice, they wanted to follow the command of Jesus that His followers deny themselves, pick up their cross, and follow Him. (See, for example, Matthew 16:24.) In light of this injunction, the Holiness people made every effort to comply with and follow the teachings of Jesus.

The Bible encourages those who pursue personal holiness with the promise of the great reward of being close to God. For example, Psalm 24:3–4 says, "*Who may ascend the mountain of the LORD? Who may stand in his holy place? The one who has clean hands and a pure heart, who does not trust in an idol or swear by a false god.*"

Holiness is an essential characteristic of those who follow God with the intention of drawing closer to Him. The enemy knows that those who are close to the Lord are more powerful and effective in their stance against him, so he sows tares of greasy grace into the church, hoping to create a chasm that can't be crossed. The enemy doesn't want the children of God to pay the price of following Him. He wants the church to look like the world and be likewise rendered ineffective.

The pursuit of personal holiness is admirable, and it's a must for anyone who wants to be something more than a typical Sunday pew-warmer. Those who genuinely desire to follow God must "die to self." The Holiness people knew this, and they were rewarded for their pursuits. The way they pressed into God with all their hearts gave birth to the most influential spiritual movement in world history: Pentecostalism. I wish I could tell you it went over flawlessly, but that would be inaccurate. Even so, this movement has produced undeniable fruit with a lasting legacy.

THE FRUITS OF THE PENTECOSTAL MOVEMENT

Despite obvious flaws, there were significant victories in Pentecostalism. There was a restoration of the doctrine of the baptism of the Holy Spirit with speaking in tongues. This doctrine included a renewed understanding of the whole spectrum of gifts of the Holy Spirit—not only tongues but also prophecy, healing, words of knowledge, miracles, signs and wonders, discerning of spirits, interpretation of tongues—and all these gifts were on display during this world-shaking movement.

Holiness gave birth to the welcoming of the Holy Spirit, and the Holy Spirit graciously released His gifts to those making a genuine, self-sacrificial effort to follow Jesus. Not only were the gifts restored, but so were evangelism and a heart for missions. Early in the Pentecostal movement, people who spoke in tongues had an understanding that they were speaking an earthly language native to a group of people somewhere on the planet. Many Pentecostals believed that if they had received the gift of tongues, they were called to go to the corresponding nation and share the gospel with the people who spoke their new language. Large numbers of believers received the gift of tongues, made their best guess as to which language they were speaking, and immediately bought a one-way boat ticket to be a missionary in the country whose people spoke that language.

They would pack their belongings in a casket with the understanding that they were not likely to return home and would be buried in that foreign land as a martyr's seed.

We now understand that tongues are not just for speaking to other people in a foreign language but constitute a gift useful in building ourselves up in the Spirit. Even so, Pentecostalism contributed significantly to a reinvigorated effort of the church to evangelize and engage in missions overseas.

Another contribution of Pentecostalism that few people realize is the major role this movement played in racial reconciliation in the United States. Pentecostals were the first to have regular worship meetings that welcomed Blacks along with Whites. The *Los Angeles Times* reported on the Azusa Street Revival, led by William Seymour, an African-American, and a white Methodist minister named Hiram Smith, describing the "[d]isgraceful intermingling of the races."[12]

It was unthinkable at the time. The institution of slavery in the United States had ended only about forty years prior. William Seymour was himself the son of a slave. To give further context and perspective, it would be nearly another six decades until President Lyndon B. Johnson would sign the Civil Rights Act of 1964, signaling the end of Jim Crow laws. The Azusa Street Mission was way ahead of its time. Pentecostals led racial reconciliation by way of the Holy Spirit decades before the secular world caught on.

All these contributions were monumental. The fruit of that mighty move is still gaining momentum to this day, more than a

---

12. Cecilia Rasmussen, "Vision of a Colorblind Faith Gave Birth to Pentecostalism," *Los Angeles Times*, June 14, 1998, https://www.latimes.com/archives/la-xpm-1998-jun-14-me-59833-story.html.

hundred years later. In spite of its phenomenal legacy, the movement was not without its moments of immaturity and eccentricity. Every movement is marked by growing pains, errors, honest mistakes, and outright works of the flesh, and Pentecostalism is no exception.

THE RISE OF MODERN-DAY PHARISAISM

Being a subset of the Holiness movement, Pentecostalism would later go beyond biblical instruction and step into legalism, judgmentalism, ignorance, and misuse of the Holy Spirit. Many times, they would attribute to the Lord things that simply were not godly.

Part and parcel of any heavy-handed "forced holiness" culture is a resulting rebellion. People may try with all their might to "become holy," to "be ye perfect," to "crucify the flesh," to "die to self." All these pursuits have great value, but if they are enforced through an authoritarian structure shored up by shame, guilt, and gossip, it becomes a recipe for disaster.

Sadly, people have tried—and are still trying—to achieve holiness and perfection on their own without the help of the glorious Holy Spirit. They try to do so without the love of God. They endeavor to subject themself to biblical standards without partnering with God. Such a quest is not only impossible but also self-destructive.

Possibly the ugliest face of religion is the result of these efforts. When you try to become like Jesus, live holy, and flee from your sin without the love of God working in your heart, you inevitably become like the Pharisees of Jesus's day. It hurts my heart even to say this, but, in some cases, Pentecostalism has sadly birthed many such works of the flesh.

WHEN YOU TRY TO BECOME LIKE JESUS,
LIVE HOLY, AND FLEE FROM YOUR SIN WITHOUT
THE LOVE OF GOD WORKING IN YOUR HEART,
YOU INEVITABLY BECOME LIKE
THE PHARISEES OF JESUS'S DAY.

Jesus showed such disdain for the Pharisees, considering their spiritual state much worse than that of prostitutes and tax collectors. To the latter group, He said, "Go and sin no more." (See, for example, John 8:1–11.) He was a "friend of sinners" (see, for example, Matthew 11:19), but when it came to *"white-washed tombs, which look beautiful on the outside but on the inside are full of the bones of the dead and everything unclean"* (Matthew 23:27), He rebuked them unreservedly for their hypocrisy. Those who were "religious" but did not know God received His most scathing critiques—the Scribes and Pharisees developed man-made rules they followed so closely, and they became arrogant, prideful, and harshly judgmental of those who failed to match their standards. These were the worst of the worst, the warts, the dogs, the lowest of the low. Jesus called them horrible names to their face: *"You snakes! You brood of vipers!"* (Matthew 23:33); He told them, *"You belong to your father, the devil"* (John 8:44). The Son of Man seemed to unload all His verbal ammo on them as though they were the very devil himself.

It grieves me that some moves of the flesh in the Holiness and Pentecostal movements have followed in the footsteps of those early Scribes and Pharisees. Glorious saints who once shined so brightly have delved deep into petty rulemaking. Some groups had their pastors sign commitment agreements saying they would not play cards or watch television and movies; others enforced dress codes for women and forbade the application of makeup. The lists of manufactured rules went on and on. Those who didn't follow these man-made rules were called "whores" or "devils." Those who didn't quickly conform to the regulated outward appearances were shamed and gossiped about. Some of the ones preaching holiness became the ugliest and most demonic representations of the church that our times have ever seen. What started as a beautiful attempt to know God and be faithful, holy, and right ended disgracefully in Pharisaical activity.

The result of *Pharisaism* is rebellion, and while rebelling against what is wrong is good, the rebels often throw the baby out with the bathwater. In the progress from Holiness to Pentecostalism and then to the Charismatic movement, we have seen a steady decline into cheap grace. Rebellion against the legalism of Pentecostalism is partly to blame. Unfortunately, today, this rebellion has taken hold in some Charismatic churches to the extent that some believers embrace various perverted activities that the Bible denounces.

DISCERNING GOOD FROM BAD

As upsetting as it is to acknowledge, the rebellion against fleshly attempts at holiness in Pentecostalism probably helped in large part to birth the greasy-grace movement. People were tired of the judgment, tired of the looks, tired of the gossip and slander, tired of the man-made rules. They wanted to forge another path.

One of the most challenging things in life is to know what to hang on to and what to leave behind. When we were growing up, our parents likely taught us plenty of good, worthwhile lessons we should remember but also some things worth forgetting. We have had mentors, teachers, coaches, and pastors who have spoken into our lives or taught us, by example, how we should be, what we should do. The challenge is to sift through these lessons and discern what should be kept and what should be rejected or perhaps followed in a modified way.

One of my favorite television shows is *American Pickers*. The hosts, experts in antiques and collectibles, have a job of traveling across America and sometimes to other countries and sifting through people's junk piles and collections in search of "the good stuff." They pick through garbage to find the gold—and are handsomely rewarded when their search pays off. Sometimes, the places they go to pick are spotless and orderly, with nice, well-kept displays. Other places are downright dangerous. They have had pieces of broken-down buildings fall on their heads; they have been scratched by rusty metal; they have had to wear safety masks; they've even had to fend off animals whose nests they disturbed in their search. And their primary task is to separate out what is good and desirable from other things that are not. They must distinguish the precious and valuable from the worthless.

In a similar way, we have to pick. Maybe our parents taught us good manners but were lazy and did not model self-discipline or industriousness. In that case, we must hold fast to proper manners while leaving laziness behind. Maybe our parents taught us healthy eating habits but displayed horrible tempers. We should model their diets but manage our tempers. A lot of life is spent figuring out what to keep and what to leave, and, to be fair, the church hasn't always done a good job of this.

Considering the Holiness movement, we should have kept up the pursuit of walking with God firmly with a clean heart. We should have left the habit of looking down on those who aren't there yet. It would have been profitable to keep the emphasis on racial reconciliation and forgotten the ban on any and all entertainment. It would have been wise to embrace the love for miracles and the other gifts of the Spirit, and to have left the garbage of harsh judgmentalism behind.

There have been times when we didn't "pick" well—and ended up hurting people in the process. This resulting hurt has created a widespread disdain for all standards and rules, and, in many cases, for authority itself. Rebellion is sometimes a fruit of the evil nature of people's hearts, but it can also be a response to bad leadership. Looking closer, leaders must examine their approach so that history does not repeat itself. A rebellion against legalism helped produce an on-ramp to greasy-grace theology. When you have experienced harsh, judgmental, love-less Pharisaism, you want anything but that. It's the worst.

FAILING TO "PICK" WELL CAN HURT PEOPLE IN THE PROCESS.

That's why Jesus couldn't stand it. He hated Pharisaism for the way it so grossly misrepresented Him. Oh, to be sure, Jesus had standards, but He also had love, true grace, and a genuine heart for the person. He didn't use shame, guilt, fear, and a written list of rules to enforce His "brand" of religion. Rather, He prompted repentance in people by His kindness. (See Romans 2:4.)

Regrettably, one could argue that greasy grace is the illegitimate child of harsh, judgmental Pentecostalism and the misguided portions of the Holiness tradition. Therefore, if we are going to criticize and, more important, get free from greasy grace, we need to know where it came from—what it formed in reaction to—and recognize own our part in advancing it. We need to "pick" through what is good in the Holiness and Pentecostal traditions without carrying along the baggage of the nasty, bitter judgmentalism that has plagued this genre of the faith.

If we are to have integrity, we must get the plank out of our own eye before seeking to remove the splinter from our brother's eye. (See Matthew 7.) We do that by developing ways to hold standards without acting like the elder brother in Jesus's parable of the prodigal son. (See Luke 15.) The truth has to be presented with love. Jesus rebuked the woman at the well and the woman caught in adultery (see John 4, 8). but He did so with love and through the leading of the Holy Spirit, not through harsh rebukes in a spirit of enforcing the rules.

AVOIDING ELDER-BROTHER SYNDROME

Most of us are probably familiar with the parable Jesus told about the so-called prodigal son. (See Luke 15:11–32.) At face value, the story illustrates the lavish love of a father for his wayward son, showing us a small picture of God's love for His sinful children. But, as Timothy Keller points out in his book *The Prodigal God,* many of us may be just as sinful, though not as overtly so, as the younger brother if we find ourselves reflected in the sulky, judgmental elder brother. The elder brother in this parable had followed the rules. The elder brother had served faithfully, and the elder brother had lived holy, but, deep inside, he resented his father and his younger brother. He harbored inner turmoil, jealousy, and bitterness. A life of holiness, purity, and separation from the world can tenderize your heart or embitter it. The elder brother stayed home but traveled the road of bitterness. He had "Elder Brother Syndrome," and so do many of us. When that is the case, "…we look at a reprobate 'sinner' and recognize his need of Jesus immediately but fail to see the need of the prideful soul sitting in the front pew week after week and year after year," as Pastor Patricia J. David puts it.[13]

Whenever the Lord has led me to walk in greater levels of holiness, I have found that the process softens my heart. In those seasons, I weep more easily and obey more quickly, and my heart reaches out to others more readily because holiness drew the Holy Spirit closer to me, and that closeness helped me to partake in the "divine nature." Through my pursuit of holiness, God gave me His heart for Him and for others.

However, at times, I have found myself slowly slipping into the elder-brother realm of bitterness. In these instances, I wonder why others don't keep the same standards I do. "Don't they have a relationship with the Lord?" I may ask. "Why are their convictions not the same as mine?" Before long, my heart begins to judge and criticize. "Why do they have a bigger ministry than I

13. Patty David, "The Prodigal Sons: The Elder Brother Syndrome," WesleyanResistance.com, January 14, 2018, https://wesleyanresistance. com/2018/01/14/the-prodigal-sons-the-elder-brother-syndrom/.

do? I see their life; their holiness is not up to par." I might judge pastors, ministry leaders, and "normal" church members for an apparent lack of effort and devotion. I might envy the blessings they were walking in, whether financial or ministerial, and say, "That minister uses foul language minutes after leaving the pulpit! I can't believe the coarse jokes he makes during his message." Or, "That pastor doesn't tithe. How is it he has a better car than mine?" Or, "These people don't seek the Lord as I do for hours a day." In these times, not surprisingly, I wasn't very pleasant to be around. My verbalized disdain for others meant I didn't have many friends. I had unknowingly slipped into the role of the elder brother.

If you consider the perspective of the elder brother, it has a certain logic. Here, this guy's younger brother goes off with the family's savings to party. In modern times, the younger brother would have headed straight for Miami, where his father's hard-earned income would fund lavish parties on a private yacht, lines of cocaine snorted off the backs or bellies of women with negotiable affections. Finally, a lifelong farm boy would have a shot at being the "cool guy." While his elder brother stays home shearing sheep, planting for harvest, and doing other strenuous physical work in the hot sun, his brother is on South Beach blowing a lifetime's worth of cash.

To add insult to injury, some scholars believe asking for an early inheritance, as the prodigal son did, was tantamount to expressing a wish that his father had died already. It was greed and disrespect to his father and family rolled into one.

The prodigal son was wasteful, licentious, and insulting. His actions were akin to spitting in the faces of his father and brother, and they were dishonoring to himself. Even so, the father did not forsake him or withdraw his love from him.

THE FATHER'S LOVE

I never really understood the love of our heavenly Father until I had children of my own. I'd describe it as discovering a type of love you didn't know you had in your heart. When you have a child, it's as if a chamber yet to be discovered opens in your heart. My love for my children was different from my love for God, romantic love, or the love of a pastime, such as playing a sport. It is a love only a parent can have. Before I was a father, I had nephews and nieces. I thought that my love for them was what my love for my own children would be like. I was wrong. It's a different kind of love, and a different level of love, that you can't know unless you feel it.

I sometimes struggle to imagine that God could possibly love me as much as I love my kids. It's admittedly a substantial overestimation of my own love and a severe underestimation of His, but that is how I sometimes feel. The love of a father for his children is unstoppable. The elder brother of the prodigal son didn't understand it.

While we Pentecostal elder brothers were measuring the length of women's dresses and drawing up contracts outlawing board games and TV, the younger brother began looking at brochures for holidays in Miami. Growing tired of the nasty attitudes and manufactured rules, he looked around, saw that life was short, and decided he wanted to live his "best life." *Enough of these religious duds*, he was thinking. *I want to enjoy life while I still can.* "You only live once" was no doubt his heart's cry.

The backlash of nasty religious people trying to be holy cannot be underestimated. It's not a good look. Holiness must be mixed with love, humility, and understanding. The call to holiness is not a call to be a police officer or a judge of others; it is a call to concern yourself with…yourself.

The wild ride in the world has its limits, its own set of rules, and some seriously negative drawbacks. The lesson the prodigal son learned quickly was that when you're in the world and you run out of money, you run out of friends. All the people who snorted lines with you that you thought were real friends are gone now, and you are feeding the pigs. If you have ever fed pigs, you know it's not a pleasant experience. Let's just say pigs lack personal hygiene and emit a strong, foul odor.

Moreover, when Jesus told the parable of the prodigal son, He did so as a Jew talking to other Jews. Today's equivalent of feeding pigs would be to clean out latrines, empty septic tanks, or live beneath a bridge and make a living as a prostitute. It was the lowest position a person could occupy.

Some people learn quicker than others. And some grow up in godly homes and stay on the right path their whole life. Praise God for those situations! Others have to learn by experience, trial and error, and even through pain and suffering. Members of the second group need to know that when the world has chewed you up and spit you out, there is a place of grace and love waiting for you. Yes, they must repent; yes, they need to have a contrite heart and recognize their wrongdoing—but there must be a place for them to go.

7

GREASY GRACE
AND FAKE HOLINESS—
TWO SIDES OF THE SAME BITCOIN

*[Martin] Luther had said that grace alone can save; his
followers took up his doctrine and repeated it word for
word. But they left out its invariable corollary,
the obligation of discipleship....The justification of the
sinner in the world degenerated into
the justification of sin and the world. Costly grace was
turned into cheap grace without discipleship.*
—Dietrich Bonhoeffer[14]

Bitcoin isn't a coin; it's a code and part of a blockchain. Sure,
it's a digital currency, but it isn't a coin. Some think it's a scam,

---

14. Bonhoeffer, *Cost of Discipleship*, 53.

and others think it's the wave of the future. It may be both or neither, but it's not a coin. Bill Gates has called it a "techno tour de force."[15]

Velveeta is a "processed cheese product." It has the word "cheese" in its description; therefore, less discerning diners may assume it has cheese in it. "After all, it says it right there on the box!" someone might argue. However, definitively, by FDA standards, it does not qualify as cheese. The name "cheese" has been used, but it isn't cheese. In the words of Judy Garland, "Velveeta: you can eat it—or wax your car with it!"[16]

Ultimately, these types of misdirection only fool those who don't dig deeper into the meaning. The same could be said for greasy-grace adherents. "The word 'grace' is on the book, or ministry name, or teaching, so it must be real grace!" Not at all. Greasy grace, cheap grace, sloppy agape…it is many things, but it is not grace. It is the Velveeta cheese of grace, and while it may seem a bit similar and have similar attributes, Velveeta "ain't" cheese, and greasy grace "ain't" grace; both are cheap and convenient knockoffs of the real thing. Using the word "grace" to legitimize their teaching and simultaneously changing its biblical meaning is the trickery that this movement is based upon.

Greasy-gracers further try to manipulate Bible-believing Christians by saying, "You are against grace? What kind of a Christian are you?" "You're under the law!" "You don't understand how *big* God's grace is." The last statement is probably true; however, the inference is not. The truth is that no one can

15. Dan Rice, "'Bitcoin is a techno tour de force' Reason 1: Open Source Technology," Medium.com, November 28, 2016, https://medium.com/@ thedrbits/bitcoin-is-a-techno-tour-de-force-reason-1-open-source-technology-98215fe95f70.
16. https://www.inspiringquotes.us/topic/9431-culinary/page:2.

understand the depth or height of any of God's characteristics. We understand "in part." (See 1 Corinthians 13:12.) Implied in the statement is that, unlike us, they understand how "big" God's grace is—and they alone hold the keys to that incredibly special revelation, which is far from true.

If you watch closely, you will see they all use the same slogans and mimic each other. It's gotten to the point that it seems they all went to the same conference to learn special phrases whereby they can defend their unbiblical views. Regardless of how they try to manipulate, what they teach is not grace. In its best form, it's a fumbled attempt to focus on the mercy of God.

> IN ITS BEST FORM, WHAT GREACY-GRACE PREACHERS TEACH IS A FUMBLED ATTEMPT TO FOCUS ON THE MERCY OF GOD.

GRACE, THE EMPOWERING FORCE

When I hear greasy-grace teachers, I think they are really trying to talk about God's goodness and mercy. The truth is, when we blow it, we need God's mercy, His kindness, and forgiveness. We need God to wipe the slate clean. It is "gracious" of Him to do that, and He does it often as long as people repent. However, true grace is an empowering force. It's not categorically forgiveness and mercy; moreover, it is a supernatural ability that lets us rise above what we could typically do. True grace gives us the ability to do things we could not do on our own.

Paul explains this often in his epistles. He said of himself that he had been given a *"grace…to preach to the Gentiles"*

(Ephesians 3:8) beyond what he could do on his own. He was given grace and had supernatural empowerment to help him do what he could not otherwise have done. Grace transforms us and lifts us, making us effective and useful in the hands of God. Through grace, we can fulfill our purpose, calling, and destiny. Grace is a force operating in us to accomplish kingdom purposes. It's not an excuse for sin and self-indulgence.

In 2 Corinthians 8, Paul talks about the grace of God given to the Macedonian churches. Was it to excuse sin? Was it to say that they didn't need to "do anything," that God loves them just the "way they were," and that there was no need to change or repent? No. Paul said in their poverty was grace to give financially *beyond their natural ability.* Humanly speaking, they could not have donated as much as they did to Paul's ministry. They were in a time of hardship in their region, and funds were lacking. For that very reason, it would have been reasonable for them to give less than they did. Despite their poverty, they stepped into a supernatural grace that allowed them to give beyond what they usually could. Grace is an empowering force. It's not a self-congratulating excuse factory that simultaneously spits out reasons why they don't have to do anything and how fantastic they are for not doing it.

FAKE HOLINESS

In the same way that cheap grace is not grace, fake holiness is also not holiness. Conversely, they are quite the opposite. Greasy grace is an enabling force and not empowering one. Also, fake holiness is a manmade attempt to be holy that inevitably ends in Pharisaism and uber unholiness, as we have talked about. Actually, religious sin is probably the darkest of all sins, and it flourishes in the fake holiness camp. As mentioned before, fake holiness is a major reason for the existence of cheap grace in the first place.

The fake holiness movement, although it is less widespread than the greasy-grace movement, seeks to "call out" those who engage in the sins they find particularly offensive. In many cases, it is advanced by Facebook "preachers" and "prophets" who go on "fruit-inspection" rampages. They try to publicly correct people they have no authority over, often based on sparse information of questionable accuracy that they discovered through natural means but claim to have "downloaded" in a "prophetic dream." Some will conspire with multiple fellow Facebook "preachers" to do their own hokey version of Pentecostal cancel culture and drag this preacher or that minister through the mud. It's Jerry-Springer-meets-a-really-angry-and-fleshly-Pentecostal-holiness-mob. And the target they call out is usually someone with a far greater influence than theirs, since slandering anything less than a well-known preacher wouldn't earn them any attention. Such is the nature of their desperate attempts to secure the limelight. When they are not publicly slandering people and making up lies, this group takes it upon themselves to make up rules and restrictions that aren't found anywhere in the Bible. They are a law unto themselves. And they're a train wreck.

In the same way that greasy-grace preachers have twisted the gospel message for their own perverted ends, heralds of fake holiness twist the beautiful idea of sacred consecration, perverting it into a fleshly attempt to earn grace while making themselves the self-appointed holiness police over others. Many of them are professional gossips in religious cloaks, simply put.

Judgment Day will be rough on them. I encourage you to stay away.

Personal holiness is never about calling out others; it's about calling out yourself. And at the opposite end of the spectrum to fake holiness, greasy grace seems to grant a license to engage in the worst parts of secular culture, the most sinful of indulgences. It follows the morality of the snowflake generation, whose highest goal is to avoid hurting anyone's feelings. Because they believe telling the truth—the truth that could set people free—would offend or risk hurting feelings, they back off from the truth in the name of "grace," or "love," all the while practicing perverted forms of true grace and love.

Such actions bow down and kiss the ring of culture. Fake holiness is quite the opposite; it is an attempt to reject culture and run from it. As Bible-believing, Jesus-following evangelicals and Spirit-filled Christians, we cannot bow to culture, but we also should not run away from it. We must engage with it while maintaining our biblical standards as we seek to live out the injunction to be "in the world but not of it." (See John 17:11, 14–15.) How can we be as salt and light to our generation if we refuse to engage with people and set for them an example worth emulating? (See Matthew 5:13–16.)

During Jesus's dinner at the Pharisee's house, a prostitute washed His feet and kissed them. (See Luke 7:37–39.) Jesus didn't run from her because she was unclean, nor did He run from the Pharisees. His presence prompted the ungodly to repent and exposed the ungodliness in the Pharisee. We must be in the world and not of it, but greasy grace and fake holiness keep us either of the world (greasy grace) or out of the world (fake holiness). These movements are two sides of the same counterfeit coin. They have both missed the mark because they are carnal attempts to achieve what only the Spirit of God can produce: true holiness, costly grace.

These two are strange bedfellows, to be sure. Greasy grace accepts too much and is too permissive, while fake holiness rejects too much and enforces uptight rules that the Bible never put forth. Both are self-righteous, and both are wrong.

DANGEROUS DITCHES

Where I grew up, in Alvin, Texas, we got a lot of rain. At one time, my hometown set a record for rainfall: in 1979, Tropical Storm Claudette brought in 43 inches of rain in 24 hours, the most ever recorded in the United States. The record still stands today. I was there in that rainstorm as a young boy.

Though 43 inches in 24 hours was a highly unusual amount, there is always a lot of rain in that region. It is a subtropical climate with alligators, palm trees, and mosquitoes the size of hummingbirds. With all that water, there has to be a sound water management system in place. In some parts of town, like the street I grew up on, there were drainage cellars that would collect the runoff. However, just around the corner and down a bit, there were ditches on either side of the road that would help manage the massive amounts of water that would sometimes flow through.

These ditches were a great source of fun when we were kids. When it rained, they were the closest thing we had to a swimming pool. One of my friends had a really large drainage ditch in front of his house and a smaller side ditch that ran the length of his property perpendicular to the larger ditch. Together, the two ditches form a T shape. When it rained heavily, we would run down the side ditch, then jump and slide headfirst into the main ditch.

In these ditches, we would look for snakes and crawdads, and sometimes we would swim through the culverts sitting below the driveway entrances to the homes. What were solid water-management systems to the city works department of Alvin, Texas, were tons of fun for us kids.

When the ditches were dry, we would use them as forts for playing cowboys and Indians with our bows and rubber-tipped arrows and plastic guns. They were a great place to hide during a game of hide-and-seek, and their inclined shape served as a perfect bike ramp where you could "catch some air."

When I was a kid, these ditches were some of the best places to play, but they also served as a warning. At fifteen, when I started learning how to drive, those ditches were no longer enticing. On the contrary, I avoided them at all costs, desperate to keep my $1,200 Datsun 210 on the road. One wrong move, and my car could be in the ditch, and I would be demoted from driving a car to pedaling around on my bicycle—not a good look for a teenager. This fun place of play became a place of concern as I grew into my driving years. It was a great picture for life. There are ditches on both sides of the road, and I need to be careful.

As we have seen, the pendulum has swung from holiness attempted in the flesh alone to greasy grace that says you can do whatever you want and never have to worry about judgment. As we journey forward in our pursuit of God, we will find a "ditch" on either side of the road: grace and judgment, licentiousness and holiness. In one ditch is an overemphasis on God's mercy and kindness, which, if misunderstood, might send us tumbling headlong into greasy grace. In the other ditch is the effort to walk in holiness of our own ability, without relying on and partnering with the Lord, which leads us into the dark, Pharisaical realm of fake holiness. We have to watch ourselves. We have to keep our hearts pure and our path close to the Lord. This walk with God is flanked by two ditches, and wisdom calls us to proceed with caution.

Let's choose the narrow path and stay out of the ditches.

8

WEEDING OUT THE TELLTALE TALK OF CHEAP GRACE

For they mouth empty, boastful words and, by appealing
to the lustful desires of the flesh, they entice people who are
just escaping from those who live in error.
—2 Peter 2:18

As a child, I would sometimes venture up to Amarillo, Texas, in the summer to spend time with my grandparents. My grandfather took good care of his lawn and held a particular disdain for dandelions. He liked his manicured lawn of beautiful green grass and didn't want those weeds messing up his beautiful display of green perfection. My duty as his grandson was to take a tool and dig up those dandelions by the roots. This tool looked like a screwdriver with a forked V-shape at the tip.

The process of ridding the beautiful lawn of those yellow intruders went as follows: (1) Take said screwdriver-like object in hand. (2) Locate the offending weed. (3) Unceremoniously plunge the screwdriver-like object into the ground just deep enough to get under the root and uproot that devil from the beautiful green grass. The entire process took time, focus, and sweat, but the rewards—typically ice cream and/or cash bonuses—made it worthwhile.

In the same way, we must hunt out the weeds that have infested church doctrine and teaching. It's interesting to note that, viewed up close, dandelions are actually quite beautiful; when they sprout into seed, it's fun to blow the delicate seedlings into the wind and watch them drift away. Dandelions are also edible (I'm told they make a delicious salad). These plants have many desirable characteristics, but in the end, they are still weeds that will overtake a lawn if left untreated. The theological constructs of greasy grace might seem appealing for a time, but in the end, they are weeds in the garden of the Spirit, and they must be uprooted.

To properly hunt these greasy-grace weeds, we can't use a V-shaped tool as I did with the dandelions in my grandparents' yard. We have to use the Word of God, plunging that two-edged sword directly into the deceptions of greasy-grace theology. We have to clear those lovely-seeming weeds out of the pure green grass of the gospel.

RECOGNIZING THE MENACE OF TWISTED TRUTH

Some of the lofty platitudes of greasy-grace terminology "sound" right and good; like the dandelion weed, they may even "taste" okay. "God's grace and love are so big"; "His love is so wonderful"; "He isn't a judge; He's a cuddly daddy"; "Jesus paid it all"; "Jesus said it is finished!"; "God is 'cool' with our sins or 'bigger' than our sins." These statements are not outright lies. The enemy's oldest trick is to twist the truth. He did it with Eve in the garden of Eden, and he did when he tempted Jesus in the wilderness. In the same way, greasy-gracers twist the Scriptures to bolster their ideas. They use the credibility that Scripture carries to give credence to their false teachings.

One of the biggest challenges to people swayed by the greasy-grace message is that what greasy-grace preachers teach is partially true. Greasy-grace preachers don't deal in outright lies; no, they realize people are too aware to fall for them. They have to be cunning and deceptive to fool people. Instead of dealing in outright lies, they deal in half-truths. Sadly, many unlearned or less discerning believers go right for the cheese and fall for the mouse trap of greasy grace.

JESUS'S WORK MAY WELL BE FINISHED, BUT OURS IS JUST BEGINNING.

Yes, Jesus did say, "It is finished." (See John 19:30.) That isn't the problem. The greasy-grace interpretation of His statement is the problem. Greasy-grace preachers argue that because Jesus said, "It is finished"—because "He paid it all"— we are completely free from any duties or responsibilities. They assert that because Jesus gave up His life as a sacrifice for our sins, we aren't required to do anything except, of course, "relax." Such teachers twist the Scriptures and biblical principles for the purpose of coddling the flesh. They teach that because Jesus died, we don't need to do anything but receive that gift. But Jesus said quite the opposite. His work may well be finished, but ours is just beginning.

WHAT JESUS REALLY SAID ABOUT THE CHRISTIAN LIFE

Jesus calls us, for example, to deny ourselves, take up our crosses, and follow Him. (See Matthew 16:24; Mark 8:34.) He calls us to repent and turn from our sins. (See, for example, Matthew 4:17.) Greasy-grace preachers will tell you there is no need to repent because "Jesus paid it all!" Yes, but even after He did so, He was still calling for the church to repent. Following His death and resurrection, He spoke through John the revelator, exhorting the church to confess their sins and turn from them, lest they subject themselves to judgment. (See, for example, Revelation 2:5, 16.) Jesus held the church to a standard. He told them where they were right and where they were wrong, and He had great expectations for those who were called by His name.

Greasy-grace proponents will tell you that you don't need to fast. They will tell you that disciplines such as fasting are "works" that are based in the law that Jesus's death abolished. This type of teaching indicates either biblical ignorance or a willful disobedience of Scripture. Jesus said, "*When you fast…*" (Matthew 6:16). The implication is that believers should be fasting. This practice isn't optional; it's expected. Jesus said that when the bridegroom is gone, there will be fasting, meaning that after He ascended, His followers would fast. (See Mark 2:19.) Another greasy-grace dandelion plucked out of the green grass of truth.

As another example, many greasy-grace teachers will tell you that the practice of tithing is "operating under the law" and that we should give according to how we "feel." This flies in the face of what Jesus taught in such verses as Matthew 23:23 and Luke

11:42. Yet greasy-gracers are a law unto themselves. They haven't studied the Bible, they have ignored what they have studied, or they argue that the Bible doesn't mean what it says. They stretch, contort, manipulate, and twist God's Word until it is unrecogniz-able. They aren't subject to God's Word; they subject God's Word to their whims. In doing so, they use sleight of hand to twist their way out of anything "unpleasant," while accusing anyone who fol-lows God's Word in that regard of being "religious."

WHAT JESUS REALLY SAID ABOUT HELL

Probably the darkest lie promoted by greasy-grace theology is the idea that hell doesn't exist. Jesus said just the opposite. He spoke of a harsh, never-ending eternal judgment for those who don't believe in Him. Yet the greasy-grace crowd sidesteps this truth by saying, "A loving God wouldn't send people to hell; what kind of narcissist is the God you serve? I serve a God of love, peace, and forgiveness, not that meanie 'religious' God of the Bible."

One thing I would point out—something you may have already noticed—is that all of the completely unbiblical view-points brought about by the promoters of greasy grace have to do with things that most people find hard, unpleasant, or uncomfortable. The things they hate are things that cost, and they loathe the aspects of the Christian life that demand duty and responsibility.

Greasy-gracers are so desperate to sound "nice" and con-genial, but once you've boiled down their beliefs to their basic form, what they amount to is the idea that Jesus's work was so powerful, and His grace is so good, that we don't have to do anything we don't feel like doing.

For those who have eyes to see, this is clearly a deceptive smokescreen used by those who are unwilling to pay the price of following the Lord Jesus. These people want to explain away the difficult parts, so as not to discomfort or inconvenience themselves in any way. This dandelion gospel must be taken out by the root. If you have been deceived by the lies of cheap-grace preaching, you must pluck them out one by one with the truth of God's Word and be set free from the bondage of those lies.

UNDERSTAND THE POWER OF WORDS

Anytime you want to undo a lie, using correct terminology is a good approach. Jesus Himself fought the devil with words. (See Matthew 4; Luke 4.) The enemy uses words, and we need to use words when we encounter him. Secular psychologists take a similar approach, helping their clients to use words to frame their thoughts, emotions, and ideas. They use terminology and phrases to help buffer concepts and reinforce ideas, which is a powerful tool and a helpful strategy that should be applied when undoing false teachings and theologies.

When you have truth and revelation, it's also helpful to bring language to those truths. It's a valuable gift to the body of Christ when God blesses people with the gift of communication, whether verbal, written, or other means. Being able to express concepts and ideas coming from God is an invaluable gift to the church.

On the contrary, when the enemy sows a lie through false teachers, the terminology and phrases they use can be a powerful tactic to deceive. People are susceptible to smooth talkers, slick lingo, and well-presented thoughts. Many times, a charismatic teacher, sometimes even a charismatic leader with good intentions, will twist the Word of God to make it fit his own agenda. At this point, the Bible is no longer used as God's living Word to correct and shape, rebuke, and encourage; no, now, the Bible is a tool that is warped to get the desired end. We have to ensure that the teachers we listen to not only quote the Word of God but "rightly divide" it, as well. (See 2 Timothy 2:15 NKJV, KJV.) Remember, even the devil knew the Word of God and quoted it. (See, for example, Matthew 4:6.)

BE WARY OF THOSE WHO PRIORITIZE "BEING NICE"

Being "nice" and speaking to others accordingly is thought to be the ultimate virtue within the cheap-grace movement. This fact is foundational to understanding the mental framework of those who subscribe to that movement. This mindset parallels the modern spirit that says if you don't agree with someone, you are full of "hate" or that you're being a "bully." While it's true that hatred and bullying are widespread in the world, the mere instance of a disagreement does not automatically qualify as such. It's simply a cheap manipulation trick used pretty effectively these days on the less discerning. A good copy of *Webster's* dictionary could solve a lot of today's problems. So could—big surprise!—a healthy dose of Scriptures. For example, Proverbs 27:6 (NKJV) says, *"Faithful are the wounds of a friend, but the kisses of an enemy are deceitful."*

In greasy-grace circles, "playing well with others" and being "agreeable" are part and parcel of the highest ethos. A generation ago, we valued "tough love," directness, and honesty. Within the span of a generation or two, we have prioritized coddling people's feelings over telling them a hard but ultimately beneficial truth.

From where did this new value system come? How did we go from my grandfather's generation of looking a man in the eye, having a firm handshake, abiding by your word, and being a person of honor, to just telling people whatever they want to hear, no matter how ridiculous it sounds? It's strange to think how a culture could become so deluded and slip so far into falsehood in just a few generations.

A LOST REVERENCE FOR THE WORD OF GOD AND A CORRESPONDING DEVALUATION OF THE MALE

From a spiritual standpoint, the embracing of falsehood in the church comes in large part from a lack of love for the Word of God. This decline in honoring God's Word has led to a degradation of traditional moral values.

One regrettable downward shift in values came from dishonoring the male contribution in our culture. Today, if you turn on a sitcom, you find reruns of the blundering deliveryman on *King of Queens*; his wife, who has it "together," is the brains and pants of the operation. If you switch the channel (admittedly, it's been a while since I have watched TV) to *Everybody Loves Raymond*, you have an overbearing wife barking orders at her dimwitted dolt of a husband. His life is torture because his wife is smart, capable, bossy, and mean, while he is a bumbling idiot forced to snap to attention at her command. There seems to have been a whole generation of sitcoms with a similar premise: attractive, smart woman has to put up with the buffoonery of her funny but clueless husband.

I'm not saying that there aren't any men like that in real life, nor am I saying that it's never okay to portray males in those ways. In this nation, we have freedom of speech, and people can do as they wish. If you turn back the hands of time, you see women being portrayed as weak and dimwitted on such shows as *I Love Lucy*. Lucille Ball was forever needing her cool, calm, collected husband to get her out of her latest jam. Such comedic portrayals can be okay until they are the sole ways that either sex is represented.

Today, there seems to be an almost default disrespect for men. "Too much testosterone in the room" is a common pejorative statement against men that, interestingly, is never used when witty comments are made, intellectual ideals are discussed, or brave actions are taken. It is reserved for men displaying typical male characteristics of strength that may be misconstrued for aggression or traditional attitudes and behaviors. Men are called "oppressors," even though it was men who recognized the need for equality and gave women the right to vote and work in America. Leftists and feminists slanderously refer to American culture as having a "rape" culture. They say this as though part and parcel of our cultural values are pursuant to promoting rape instead of some outliers working against the system for their own perversions and sense of power. Further, in the same line of male disrespect, although it's changing now somewhat, divorce courts almost always favor women for child custody. Still, by and large, it isn't that men are oppressed; it's just that more of a negative cultural attitude against men is pervasive.

While there is always a need to strive for equality, toxic feminism has so interwoven its power-grasping ideology into the fabric of our society that the need for male leadership is no longer honored. This is true in many cases, even among people who claim to be Bible-believing Christians. The idea of headship or a male leadership role in the family would elicit a series of strong gasps from the "woke" members of our churches. That is probably the reason why many men are leaving their families—the Western worldview has eliminated the man's place of honor and respect. Why would someone remain where he is repeatedly dishonored, and where the surrounding culture condones such treatment? This is not an excuse for a man to leave his family; quite the opposite: true grace allows us to overcome even the most difficult of circumstances. However, while this is not an excuse, it is often a reason why. We must come to the place again where we give honor to the men in our culture.

In general, men value respect, and women value love. Admittedly, there are other reasons for separation and divorce, but it is true that many men ultimately leave their homes because they are not honored in their households. Like the sitcoms, they are reduced to the role of the one who is always wrong, always screwing up, and never good enough. These toxic feminist ideologies and rebellion often usurp their place as head of the family and many other aspects of our culture. Many women do not see themselves as being disrespectful or dishonoring men, but our culture encouraged a lack of respect of men to the point where disrespect of traditionally masculine or male characteristics seems "normal."

This prevalent dishonor of men in our culture has played a significant role in the shifting of societal values. It seems that, to a significant degree, Western culture embraces feminine values—and immediately calls out and criticizes the assertion of so-called masculine values. Little thought is given to this dangerous dynamic. Of course, this is not to say we shouldn't esteem "feminine" values; we simply should not do so to the point of suppressing or utterly excluding "masculine" values. We need a healthy balance of the two, not the exaltation of one and the dishonoring of the other. Yet the latter is the regrettable path our culture has taken. As a result, we lack a proper balance because we fail to embrace traditionally masculine values along with their feminine counterparts.

A PREVALENCE OF SINGLE-PARENT FAMILIES

Part of the problem is that many people have grown up in single-family homes where the mother was the only leader of the family. Now, a mother's contribution to the raising of her children is priceless—I won't deny that. The nurture, warmth, gentleness, and patient care of a good mother are fundamental components of a child's healthy growth and development. Tender kisses of bumps and bruises, reassuring hugs after a bad dream, snacks of warm cookies and cold milk—all these and more are cherished, priceless expressions of a mother's love for a child. Those of us who were raised by good, faithful mothers will tell you there is no love like a mother's love. However, it was never intended for a mother to raise her children on her own. A mother's love, as valuable as it is, remains incomplete without the love of a father.

That's not to say that fathers can't kiss wounds, give hugs, offer bottles of milk, and provide other measures of comfort. Sure, a father can encourage, coddle, and love. I do it for my daughters. In the same way, a mother can discipline, give advice, counsel, set expectations, and fulfill other roles traditionally assigned to the father. There are no hard-and-fast rules regarding the roles of a mother or father dictating what either parent must do. Individual cultures and personalities play a huge part in determining how people parent. But, generally speaking, a father's contribution is different from a mother's, and vice versa.

A father often has strengths and capabilities that a mother may lack or possess to a lesser degree. Both parents' unique sets of gifts and contributions, though of equal importance, may not always be similar. Neither one is more important than the other, but if one is missing, the child's development may be compromised by additional problems than those faced by a child with both parents in the home. We see this played out in crime and poverty statistics. Those without a father are more likely to be incarcerated, less likely to graduate from university, and more likely to live in poverty.[17] The mother's contribution is necessary, and so is the father's.

One area where a father's influence is particularly effective is in discipline, which helps the development of a child's moral compass, teaching the child to discern the difference between right and wrong. My kids know our family's standards. My daughter Emily, now four years old, already knows where Dad stands on most issues and has a "healthy fear" of me. If she blows it, she knows she will be punished appropriately. We have a warm and loving relationship, and a day doesn't go by that we don't hug each other or tell each other, "I love you." At the same time, Emily knows who lays down the law, and she doesn't want to cross it. I'm not saying that a mother doesn't contribute to her child's moral compass. She does. And every family is different. But, in my experience, children will push their mother's boundaries, but they know they're in real trouble when they hear, "Wait until your dad gets home." Men have a natural grace for guiding the development of this moral compass if they lead their families as they ought.

17. See, for example, Jerrod Brown, "Father-Absent Homes: Implications for Criminal Justice and Mental Health Professionals," Minnesota Psychological Association, August 4, 2021, https://www.mnpsych.org/index. php%3Foption%3Dcom_dailyplanetblog%26view%3Dentry%26category% 3Dindustry%2520news%26id%3D54.

Another area where fathers typically excel is in showing "tough love." I hate to spank my kids, ground them, put them in the corner, or take away their cherished items for a time. It really hurts my heart. I think it upsets me more than it concerns them. It's probably the most challenging part of being a father for me. Yet, sometimes, I have no choice.

For example, in our house, lying is a big deal. If you break a vase and tell the truth about it, that's no biggie. You might get a lecture about being more careful or that it isn't wise to play roller derby in the house, but there won't be any spanking, grounding, or other serious punishment. If, however, you break a vase and lie about it, there will be serious consequences. To get caught in a lie in my house is a grave issue. Honesty is one of our top values, and my wife and I work together to uphold this value. In doing this, we are setting our children's moral compasses to prioritize honesty.

My daughters are diligent students who consistently earn good grades. If either of them performs poorly on a test or otherwise fails to live up to her potential, we work with her on a strategy to do better. We start by talking to the teacher. We then look at ways my wife and I can help more with homework. We don't punish our daughters for poor grades; we look for more effective strategies to help them succeed. However, if one of our girls pushes or hits her sister, our judgment is swift. There will be tough love, and our daughters know it.

Normally, dads need to lead in establishing and enforcing family rules and values. They shouldn't be "uncle dads" primarily known for buying their kids toys and taking them to Disney World or "babysitters" for when Mom isn't available. To raise a good kid, sometimes you have to be the "bad guy." Anything less is simply enabling, which will only harm your kids in the long run. As the family leader, the man should see that his authority is communicated with clarity in his household.

When our girls were very young, we made it clear that such potentially dangerous activities as playing with electric plugs or running out into the street would result in swift punishment. These types of things might have happened once, at the most, twice. Any such instances of rule-breaking were severely punished because their very lives were at stake. We had to strongly communicate that there would be severe consequences if they crossed the lines we had established. We made good on our word and followed through with our established consequences, and they learned quickly.

The Art of Collaborative Child Discipline

These examples I have shared are simple, everyday pictures of how parents can love their children through discipline, even serious discipline. While I have no doubt that there are mothers who excel at this, discipline seems to belong traditionally to the father's domain.

I trust that the gentle reader will forgive the broad strokes I'm painting with. I know there are exceptions to these rules, even in my house; but, categorically speaking, mothers coddle, nurture, and reassure, while fathers correct, discipline, and encourage the children to grow up into their potential. In the hour we're living in, when fathers are often absent from the home, and the contributions of a father are constantly belittled and dishonored, many children receive their mothers' contribution but miss out on that of their fathers. What will they be left with without masculine input? The answer is a lopsided dose of feminine values.

"But, David!" you might protest. "Are you condemning traditionally feminine values?" Not at all. On the contrary, they are desperately needed. It's just that, as I've said, they are incomplete on their own. Sadly, in any community where most of the sons are being raised solely by their mothers, the boys often never become men. They seldom reach their potential because they aren't corrected and disciplined in the way that only a father can correct and discipline. They aren't taught to anticipate and accept the consequences of their actions. Consequently, they don't grow up. They remain as coddled babies, even into adulthood. This generation is full of "man-babies" and "woman-babies."

When a growing child brings a problem to a single mom, the mother will often follow her nature by coddling and nurturing, doing whatever she can to make the child feel better. She is not doing something wrong; this is how she was created, but she was never intended to raise a child on her own. In such a situation, when there is no dad present to speak the difficult truths, the child is likely to have his growth stunted.

Moms generally exude a feeling of warmth and security, while dads provoke growth and change. A mother's love and reassurance provide her children with the courage to accept the sometimes-difficult father-led initiatives to change, grow, push oneself, and deal with the consequences of one's wrongdoings. It is a powerful dynamic in the growth of a person. There is a synergy between the input of both parents. Without the contributions of both mother and father, a child will develop with certain essential values being overemphasized, while others are underemphasized or even neglected altogether.

Instead of accepting the challenge to look in the mirror, recognize and acknowledge one's faults, and correct one's ways, such a child will instead run to his mom. He'll ask her to kiss his boo-boo one more time, to nurture and baby him. And she will probably respond as expected, since it is how she is wired. She is doing the right thing from her abilities, but the child's development can easily take a wrong trajectory without a balanced collaboration of both parents.

The Need to "Be Nice"

I acknowledge that some women and men do great jobs as single parents. These statements are in no way made to disparage them. Most do their absolute best and should be respected and applauded for their efforts. Again, these statements are broad generalizations made to help us better understand the origins of the prized ethos of "being nice"—of avoiding offending others at all costs. This virtue is more feminine in nature. People who were raised solely by women, in fatherless households, often take on this virtue, sometimes to the exclusion of all other virtues.

We see the same dynamic appear in greasy-grace theology. Greasy grace is an effeminate theology. It's a theory that appeals particularly to those who have not been raised with a positive masculine figure in their life. For example, there are people who need to hear such hard truths as these: "Without Jesus, you will spend an eternity in hell!" or "You are lazy and need to get a job and move out of the basement!" But in greasy-grace circles, anyone who would dare to speak these difficult truths is bound to be maligned. The spoiled man-child will gravitate to the feminine virtue of "not being mean." He hasn't learned to listen to or appreciate the love-filled challenge from a father. It is unfamiliar, so he rejects it outright. He will cling to the comfort of feminine coddling when his shortcomings are discussed because that is all he knows and all he can handle. He resents men and male leadership because he has no experience with it. He develops a growing disdain for authority. Most of it is subconscious, but when you are not trained to respect, appreciate, and obey your father's authority, obeying an outsider becomes that much more difficult.

A man who was raised strictly by his mother is also likely to harbor negative impressions of men that he learned from his mother, if she was as embittered toward men as many single mothers are. The anger of a single mother who has been abandoned by her husband is often passed along to her children, sons and daughters alike. Her sons may end up hating themselves because they have been taught, explicitly or implicitly, that men are evil. Such children will not embrace the tough love that could help them grow. Rather, they are apt to seek to indulge their emotions repeatedly. In this kind of environment, there is no place for truth, growth, confrontation, or transformation. Babying one's children into adulthood causes the metamorphosis into manhood and womanhood to be delayed or even aborted. Such "adults" will remain as adolescents, mentally and emotionally.

> **BABYING ONE'S CHILDREN INTO ADULTHOOD CAUSES THE METAMORPHOSIS INTO MANHOOD AND WOMANHOOD TO BE DELAYED OR EVEN ABORTED.**

THE GENDER DEBATE AND MENTAL ILLNESS

Another arena where we see the priority of "niceness" is in today's gender debate. As I write this, I am shocked that segments of our society have led this discussion as far as it's gone. It's weird that it is even a "thing." The ludicrous, farfetched audaciousness of the basic premise of the arguments really defies words.

The basic idea is that one's gender is "whatever one 'feels' like inside." If you are a man but you "feel" like a woman, you should be considered a woman instead of just a confused man. A generation ago, this kind of talk would have gotten you a one-way ticket to the crazy house, and rightly so. If you are a man who thinks he is a woman, or even an alien or a giraffe, God still loves you. You still have intrinsic worth as a human. You still likely have other, unbelievably valuable, beneficial parts of your personhood. But you are also confused and, without question, mentally ill.

If this is the case for you, don't worry—you're in good company. Statistics show that mental illness is on the rise. Estimates are that over 50 percent of people who live in large cities have one form of mental illness or another.[18] Stress, anxiety, eating disorders, depression, and anger issues all count as mental illnesses. So, don't feel singled out. Lots of people have a mental illness, and there is a lot of help available.

That being said, you aren't "brave" for feeling like you are a woman if you are a man. You aren't a crusader, conqueror, leader, or voice of the future. Like many—like I was, at certain times in my life—you are a person in need of help. You do not deserve special rights or privileges. You are not a member of a unique group of "marginalized" people needing special treatment, recognition, or protection.

---

18. Andrea Mechelli, "Cities Increase Your Risk of Depression, Anxiety and Psychosis—but Bring Mental Health Benefits Too," The Conversation, December 18, 2019, https://theconversation.com/cities-increase-your-risk-of-depression-anxiety-and-psychosis-but-bring-mental-health-benefits-too-128911.

You should not be allowed to go into the restroom, changing room, or locker room designated for members of the opposite gender. You should not be allowed to participate in athletic events reserved for the opposite sex or force everyone else, through legal means, to indulge you in your misunderstanding of yourself. Yes, you may well believe you are a woman on the inside, but the truth remains that you are a man on the outside. I understand that you feel differently. Those feelings don't mean you are a terrible person without any value. They just mean that you are mistaken.

Some people think they are Elvis, or Abraham Lincoln, or Jesus. Thinking oneself to be someone else does not automatically make it so. Sometimes, what people think they are, and what they really are, are two different things. Such confusion happens in many facets of life and experience. Delusional thinking is not limited to those with gender dysphoria. Treatment, counseling, and other approaches can help confused individuals to deal with these issues. Lying about it and conspiring with a person in their delusion doesn't help anyone, nor is it kind. The feminine "nice guy" virtue keeps people from telling this truth because not hurting someone's feelings is, for them, a preferable course to helping someone out of their delusion.

WOUNDED-ANIMAL SYNDROME

When I was growing up, our family was good friends with our next-door neighbors. We lived pretty close to Clear Lake, Texas, where mission control for NASA was located. Michael, the father of the family, was an engineer for NASA. He was incredibly precise with everything he did. It was great to have him as our neighbor because his knowledge of aerodynamics came in very handy in our Cub Scout pinewood derby races.

If I recall correctly, both my brothers and I placed first in the competitive race. It just isn't fair going against NASA knowledge at the pinewood derby; nevertheless, we took full advantage. To this day, I still have those cars displayed on my bookshelf at home and will never forget the value of sound engineering in wooden car races.

Inside Michael's garage, he had hung a small whiffle ball from the ceiling so that his wife would know how far in to pull her car before parking. Where her windshield met the whiffle ball was the place to stop. They were a very meticulous, orderly family. What else would you expect from a member of the team who put the first man on the moon?

One day, our neighbors had some family members over. This family drove a large blue suburban. Today, those cars are still huge, but they were far and away larger than any other car on the market when they first came out. I clearly remember the behemoth 1980s gleaming blue suburban pulling into our neighbors' driveway. It was quite a sight to see. I have seen apartments in New York City that are smaller than this monstrosity of a car.

Well, on this particular day, when it was time for our neighbors' guests to leave, they started backing their huge vehicle out of the driveway. Unfortunately, another neighbor had let their dog out, and the little dog found its way under the tires of this huge car. As the vehicle backed up, there came a loud, blood-curdling yelp. The car quickly pulled forward, but the damage was done.

If the car had crushed the skull, the pain would have just been a moment for the little pooch, but fate was not so merciful to the dog. Our canine friend was a long, narrow, short dog who, sadly, had his legs and lower back crushed in the incident. This injury left him very injured but still very much alive.

The neighbors' guests left in their big blue suburban, and our NASA engineer neighbor Michael was left to clean up the mess. I was close by when Michael went over to the dog. He had something in his hand—I don't remember if it was a piece of cardboard or a stick—but he was trying to put the dog on to a makeshift cardboard mat of some sort. Presumably, he would take the dog to the vet to get medical help (or, more likely, to be put down).

I remember like it was yesterday when Michael approached the dog. I had been around that dog before. He was pretty friendly and seemed to like the people in our neighborhood in general. Typically, you could see this pup walking around and wagging his tail, almost always in a good mood. Unfortunately, all the NASA engineering in the world wasn't going to put this little pup back together again.

As soon as Michael went over to help the dog, the animal bared its teeth, giving a vicious snarl and a violent bark. When Michael tried to help the dog, the dog lashed out and tried to bite him. The animal bared his teeth again, clearly full of anger and hurt. At this point, Michael went to find the owner. I'm not sure what happened next, but I will never forget the dog's face, its teeth, and its snarl. In seconds, it went from being a friendly family pet and beloved neighborhood animal to a wounded, angry, violent creature. Why? Because it had been seriously wounded.

Today, many people are like wounded animals. Hurt by life, relationships, and/or circumstances, they are unwilling or unable to move forward. They may be harboring real hurts, or maybe they've just had typical life stuff happen to them. Either way, instead of going through the painful work of letting go and moving on, they opt for the easier route of bitterness, which then develops into a victim mentality.

When your identity is found in being a victim, there are some obvious benefits. You have built-in excuses as to why you can't succeed; any mistake you make can be blamed on somebody else. A victim starts every conversation by saying, "I'm so oppressed," or "I'm just a victim," or "I've been hurt before." One's past hurt becomes their present identity.

I don't mean to sound unsympathetic toward people who have suffered real trauma or hurt. I know life can be challenging and even downright cruel sometimes. But, as a society, I think we become enablers when we allow people to identify themselves as victims instead of helping them to live as victors.

Those with a victim mentality become like the dog that was run over by the suburban. For some people, it's understandable. Some people have lived truly tragic lives. Ministering over the last two decades, I have heard many sad stories. Some of them would make you sick to your stomach and leave your jaw hanging open. The hardships and violations some people have suffered are almost unimaginable. I heard one particularly horrific story by the well-known "Machine Gun Preacher" about child soldiers in Sudan. Sam Childers told me that these kids, in some cases, were forced to kill their own parents. It's actually happened a lot in Uganda and South Sudan in recent decades.

Our ministry has worked to rescue the victims of sex trafficking in India through the Magdalene Project. Through this ministry, I met a girl named Poojah who was sold to a brothel as a young teen by her stepmom to pay off the family debt. My team in India worked with Poojah. She is now healthy and happy, with a husband and a family of her own. She gave her life to Christ, received vocational training, and now works as a professional seamstress. We praise God for her transformation and for the child soldiers rescued by Sam Childers's ministry. At the same time, these kids' lives are a reminder that the world can be a cruel place.

When people go through unspeakable hardships and are subject to devastating injuries and deep emotional wounds, they are not likely to recover after a single counseling session or one trip to the altar. It takes real, concentrated work to overcome such immense hurts. I am not here to trivialize real pain or to dismiss people who are actual victims. However, if the worst thing that ever happened to you is someone called you by an ethnic slur, or you didn't make the basketball team, or someone called you "fat" in junior high school, then it's time to buck up and get over it. If your most scarring memory is not getting invited to the prom or losing your student-council race in junior high, you need to get beyond that. Even more hurtful things than those examples still need to be dealt with head-on. I don't want to minimize anyone's pain, but I also don't want to maximize it. We should never define our entire lives by moments, days, or weeks of hurt. Acknowledge it, find some tools or resources to deal with it, and then move forward.

Otherwise, you're apt to develop what I call "wounded-animal syndrome." To those dealing with this syndrome, everything is a hurt that reminds them of just how mean people have been to them in the past. That wounded dog didn't want help from my neighbor Michael because it was too hurt to receive help at that point. In the dog's case, it was understandable. But in many cases, it's not.

The brutal truth is that you sometimes need to hurt a bit to heal. Sometimes, you need to hear that you're overweight so you can take an honest look at your health choices. Sometimes, you need to be confronted about your spending habits before you can develop more responsible financial stewardship. Sometimes, you need to be told you are in sin so you can make better decisions and get right with God.

Greasy grace avoids tough truths because many who follow the false teachings of greasy-gracers are like wounded animals. Maybe they had a rough church experience, a harsh father, or a neglectful mother. Perhaps they were "nerdy" or socially unacceptable in their growing-up years. They didn't get invited to the dance, they weren't picked for the team, or their body type was mocked. Too fat, too skinny, too dark, too light. Or, on a more serious note, maybe they were harshly abused. Whatever the cause, they have developed an injured and brittle spirit. Such a condition is often accompanied by a spirit of rejection, an orphan spirit, and a subsequent victim mentality.

SOMETIMES, YOU NEED TO HURT A BIT TO HEAL.

Individuals with wounded hearts, bitter spirits, and an overwhelming sense of rejection easily embrace the greasy-grace gospel because they cannot hear anything negative about themselves. They want to feel perfect so that they don't have to feel the pain of looking at their own imperfections. They want to feel there are no requirements needed because making any effort brings up too much pain. They are deeply wounded.

Deep, undealt-with woundedness is the petri dish of greasy grace. Those who harbor their wounds want a God who requires nothing because they feel it would hurt too much to try again. They want a God who doesn't want them to change. Why? Because change is painful, and if you are in pain, it's hard to embrace the idea of undergoing more pain.

It is a nasty trap of the enemy, the proverbial thorn in the tiger's paw. The tiger's paw is a dilemma. The paw hurts because of the thorn, but the removal of the thorn will also be painful. So, the tiger avoids the removal of the thorn. Eventually, the thorn causes an infection, and the infection travels up the leg and ultimately kills the tiger.

Many who are called to be tigers in the kingdom will die without ever making an impact because they are not willing to endure the pain of taking out the thorn. Enabling failure rather than encouraging perseverance is prominent in the greasy-grace movement. Instead of ignoring the realities of a hell and a coming judgment, and denying the existence of any requirements of those who would follow Christ with their whole hearts, the greasy-grace tigers leave the thorn in the paw.

Yet those who have been "run over" by the big blue suburban of life must allow the Lord to take the thorn out of their paw. It will hurt, certainly, but only for a season; and, by suffering that temporary hurt, they will save themselves a lifetime of pain and an eternity of misery.

It takes a secure person to admit they need improvement, to understand that love empowers the change required to walk with God. God is in the transformation business. Repeating over and over again how much you are "loved," and telling yourself that nothing can be added to what Jesus has done, is incomplete. You *are* loved, but you also need to grow and change. Love and growth aren't enemies; they are friends, partners, working hand in hand, empowering each other.

It's true that you can't add to what Jesus has done. You can't add to the perfect work that He did on the cross, nor should you try to. Jesus's sacrifice was once and for all, for all. We can add nothing to that work, but we *can* respond to it. We *can* receive it! In fact, true love requires a response. So does true grace.

When we have encountered the grace of God—when we have a revelation of Jesus's sacrifice on the cross, when we really and truly receive a baptism of the glorious Holy Spirit—we change, and we change drastically. Our old man is dead, and our new man has come. Our life is not the same; we are born again. At the end of the day, a genuine work of grace requires a response, or there is no work of grace, no revelation of the cross, nor a true baptism of the Holy Spirit. We must be born again.

RESTORING THE VIRTUE OF TRUTH-TELLING TO ITS PROPER PLACE

This is why we can't afford to prioritize being "nice" and coddling others' feelings. We must commit to telling the truth, even when the truth hurts—so that people can walk in freedom. To do this, we have to embrace traditionally masculine values, including tough love, straight talk, discipline, and honesty.

One of my favorite verses is Proverbs 27:6: *"Faithful are the wounds of a friend, but deceitful are the kisses of an enemy"* (NASB). Friends, including fathers, will faithfully wound you. Yes, they will listen to your problems; yes, a faithful friend will hug you when you cry and encourage you when you are feeling low. But, after that, a real friend will speak the truth, even if that truth could potentially wound your pride. As a culture, we are lousy at embracing the "wounding truths" that could set us free.

Does that mean we should be rude to everyone, careless with people's feelings, obnoxious, and arrogant? Not at all. In every way, where we can be truthful, we should also be kind. In every way where we can be gentle and mercy-driven, we should be. But we cannot sacrifice truth on the altar of "being a nice guy." We have to hold kindness and honesty as valuable virtues that are sometimes in tension with each other. I believe God can work in our hearts to help us be loving and kind, as well as completely honest.

With that being said, I would rather have friends who will "faithfully wound" me rather than those who would give me deceitful kisses. I would rather be offended with the truth than patted on the back and lied to with kisses as I go headlong down a self-destructive path. I love and cherish kindness and gentleness, but I also so highly value the truth. I even value truth to the point that I often look and seek out people who will be honest with me, even if their honesty might prove a bitter pill I will have to swallow. To put it succinctly, we should love people enough to tell them the truth.

Those of us who follow Jesus do so because someone was bold enough to tell us the truth. They told us that we were sinners in need of a Savior. They told us that we needed change. They were so bold as to let us know that we weren't okay the way we were, and that we needed to repent. Hopefully, they laid out this truth with love and kindness in their heart and life. Regardless, the boldly spoken truth is irreplaceable and must be present, or it is not the true gospel.

In its true form, the gospel of Christ is confrontational. The gospel reminds us that we can't find God without Christ. The gospel message is clear that we are in sin, and we desperately need to change. It tells us to repent, to live differently. The gospel doesn't coddle your emotions, nor does it tell us that we're okay when we're not.

The gospel gives us the power to be changed, transformed, forgiven, and to grow in God. It is the true gospel. Jesus loves everyone the way they are, but He loves them too much to leave them the way they are.

We should embrace the values of kindness and mercy, but we can't afford to prize being the "nice guy." Sometimes, we have to love someone enough to tell them things they don't want to hear. True grace revels in the freedom-bringing truth and displaces being a "nice guy" as the highest virtue.

9

GETTING OUR MINDS RIGHT AND EXPOSING THE ENEMY'S SCHEMES

Those who live according to the flesh have their
minds set on what the flesh desires;
but those who live in accordance with the Spirit have their
minds set on what the Spirit desires.
—Romans 8:5

Scripture teaches that born-again believers have at work within their hearts two adversarial forces: the flesh and the Spirit. The flesh is the "old man," the part of our hearts and minds that wants to do wrong, that's inclined to sin. As we see here in this text from Romans 8, it stems from our mindset.

Looking deeper into the original language, we see that the author, Paul, utilized the Greek word *phroneó*, which means to "think" or to "direct the mind to."[19]

So, the battle between flesh and Spirit—between pleasing God or pleasing the enemy—determines the direction in which we set our mind. We are called to do the will of the Father, but in order to do so, we cannot set our minds on the sinful desires of our flesh; we must set our minds on those things that please the Father, that welcome the great Spirit of God.

Sin is as natural in the heart of man as a fish in water. We are naturally given to sin, for we were born with a sinful nature. Even after we have been born again into the kingdom of God, that sin nature creeps up and must be resisted; Scripture directs us to "put it to death." (See Colossians 3:5.) We must refocus our thoughts away from sinful desires and focus them on the will of God.

If we are going to take this charge seriously, we must also take seriously the repercussions that result from a failure to proactively direct the focus of our minds. There are eternal consequences of the gravest nature at stake. If we fix our minds to serve the Lord with all our hearts, we will bear fruit—lasting, eternal fruit. The kingdom will be preached, and God's glory will be released. Yes, there will be suffering, and there will likely be uncomfortable moments or seasons in your life. We have to deny ourselves, crucify our flesh, take up our cross, and follow Him, but the reward is always worth it with God. (See Luke 9:23.)

---

19. *Strong's* #5426, *phronéo*, https://biblehub.com/greek/5426.htm.

If the enemies of God do not want to see the work of the kingdom and its blessings and freedom advancing throughout the world, what do they do? How do they try to stop it? If I were the devil and knew I couldn't overpower the saints of God, that I couldn't win in a direct fight, what would I do? As underpowered in the conflict as the devil is, he cannot secure victory by his strength, so he must deceive. The only tactic the enemy can use to derail the saints of God is to deceive them.

EXPOSING THE ENEMY'S TRICKERY

This deception from the enemy goes all the way back to the book of Genesis. In the garden of Eden, the snake managed to undermine Eve's trust in God by first questioning what God had said. "Did God really say you shouldn't eat any fruit?" he asked Eve. "Are you sure that is what God said?" (See Genesis 3:1.)

The same thing happens in greasy grace. "Are you sure the Bible says hell exists?" some pastors ask. "Are you sure that's what it meant? It could have been talking about Gehenna, the physical location in the valley surrounding Jerusalem, rather than a place of eternal suffering." "Did God really say…?" It's the same old lie.

After that, the devil moved to a strategy of accusation. As outrageous as it sounds, he accused God of withholding something good from Adam and Eve. "God doesn't want you to eat the fruit because doing so will make you like Him," he told Eve. (See Genesis 3:4–5.)

The enemy always tries to convince people that they would be better off without God, that God has a wrong agenda against them. The devil tries to lure people into believing that if they follow God, they will be missing out on a preferable alternative. "Don't deny yourself," the enemy says. "God is just trying to kill your fun, your potential, and your enjoyment."

We see a similar lie in the teachings of greasy grace, which insist that God is so loving, He couldn't possibly have meant what He said when He spoke on such topics as hell. "Did God truly say there was a hell?" cheap-grace preachers ask. "Where in the Scriptures does God say that hell is eternal? If He says 'eternal,' does He really mean 'eternal'? Are you sure God definitely says that?"

If you don't go along with these types of questions from greasy-grace preachers, they will proceed to the next step and accuse you, just like the serpent did in the garden of Eden. They'll keep coming at you with their weak defenses. "You just don't understand how big God's grace is." "You have a limited view of Jesus's work on the cross." "You are so religious and narrow-minded!" Because there is no clear biblical path to their false theologies, they use theological gymnastics, paired with shaming and other manipulative tactics, to reinforce their point.

ESCAPING THE GRADUAL SLIP INTO UNBELIEF

The greasy-grace doctrine largely stems from what is probably the most foundational sin: unbelief. Unbelief causes us to question God, ignore the Bible's teachings, or, even worse, twist the Scriptures for our manipulative purposes.

Those who question, twist, and ignore Scripture today are similar to the seven sons of Sceva mentioned in the book of Acts. These men were trying to drive out evil spirits from people by invoking the name of Jesus, but their motives were not pure; they used Jesus's name in a self-aggrandizing effort to gain profit, fame, a sense of power. These seven sons of Sceva tried to apply a methodology without connectedness to God. They had heard and seen enough to know who Jesus was, but they had not submitted their lives to Christ. They had the form, but no relationship with Christ was made.

The mentioning of Sceva in the Bible creates some intrigue because this man is referred to as a Jewish "high priest" in Acts 19:14, yet scholars note that there was no high priest in Jerusalem by that name, so this issue has caused some confusion.[20] Further study suggests that Sceva may have used this title in an unofficial manner, much like an honorary doctorate that is conferred today by a university. He was not a high priest in the traditional sense. He was not a high priest in the temple, but some believe that the Zadokite clan may have taken this title as an unofficial or honorary one, and it might explain where some refer to priesthoods tracing back to Zadok. But it is uncertain. In parallel, it should also be noted that the teachers in the Qumran community were referred to as the "sons of Zadok."[21]

I think honorary titles are fine, as long as they are used correctly. I have one, and I appreciate the thoughtfulness of the university that bestowed it upon me. Still, I don't walk around forcing everyone to call me "doctor." Sometimes, when people play fast and loose with titles, finding their identity or

---

20. *Barnes' Notes on the Bible*, Acts 19:14, https://biblehub.com/commentaries/acts/19-14.htm.
21. The Society for Old Testament Study, "Zadok," https://www.sots.ac.uk/wiki/zadok/.

importance in them or seeking them out, it can provide insight into their character. Perhaps Sceva was like many "bishops," "apostles," or "doctors" of today whose titles sound more impressive than their ministries actually are. Maybe Sceva was not a high priest, but, boy, did he love the title. What else can we learn about Sceva?

Scholars also confirm that he was like a traveling exorcist and had been doing this for a while. God blessed him with seven sons, so it seemed to be the family business—whether legitimate ministry or a dramatic sham, we don't know. What we do know is that the sons of Sceva didn't come to Jesus trying to learn from Him, nor did they submit to Him or honor Him. They simply wanted to use Him, both His name and authority. They wanted to add His name to what they were doing, but they didn't want to conform to Him or His leadership fully. They desired access to His tactics for their benefit, but they didn't really want to know Him.

I see the same thing in the greasy-grace movement, with many preachers trying to add Jesus to what they are already doing. Like the seven sons of Sceva, they see Jesus as a way of getting what they want more quickly. They saw it working for Jesus and His followers, so they say, "Let's dollop a bit of that 'Jesus sauce' on what we've already got going." It isn't about a heart commitment to Jesus; it's about a means to an end. It's about an opportunity.

People who hunger for the limelight, hoping to appear "enlightened" or to sell a book, often want to use the name of Jesus to accomplish their agenda and their plan. Sceva and his sons were traveling exorcists. Maybe they really wanted to help people, or perhaps they wanted to be effective. They likely had ulterior motives, but also it is possible they didn't. Perhaps they had seen people tormented by evil spirits and wanted to help them. Regardless of their motives, they knew this name of Jesus was just the "abracadabra" they needed, and they went for it.

What they didn't understand is that everything in the kingdom of God operates by faith. If you want to receive salvation, you must have faith. If you're going to experience physical healing, you must have faith. If you desire to please God, the Bible teaches that you must have faith to do it. The sons of Sceva had the form, the right words, the technique, and maybe even the right hearts, but they did not have faith.

Faith is such a powerful component. Conversely, unbelief is horrifically detrimental. Jesus could not do many miracles in His hometown of Nazareth because of the people's unbelief. (See Matthew 13:57–58.) Unbelief is such a stifling force that literally stopped the work of Jesus in its tracks.

RECOGNIZING SCHEMERS OF UNBELIEF

Today, unbelief takes many forms. The greasy-grace movement takes the form of flatly denying what Scripture says or twisting it beyond recognition. The Bible says that faith comes by hearing the Word of God (see Romans 10:17), but when we ignore God's Word, we lose faith, and when we lose faith, we are powerless.

Like the sons of Sceva, greasy-gracers have the form down; they have the correct graphics, sermon titles, and wire-rimmed glasses that express "warmth and understanding." They have the fake smile required for church life. Living on platitudes and grand ideas, they lack substance, depth, and truth. Like Sceva's boys, they're "all hat and no cattle."

Unbelief takes many forms but always leads to the wide road of destruction. Those who deny foundational scriptural truths like the reality and eternity of hell, and the need to repent, fast, and pray will fall into unbelief. Such will not win the lost, build great churches, pursue a more profound relationship with God, or dig deeper into His Word. It is a slow process of slipping away.

Like a light on a dimmer switch slowly turning off, these modern-day sons of Sceva will have their hindquarters kicked in by the enemy. Before long, they will be asking themselves, "Why do I need to go to church? Jesus can meet me right here." Soon, prayer will cease, Bible study will stop, and genuine faith will be run out of town, fleeing naked and wounded, like Sceva's boys.

I've always said that the best remedy for the greasy-grace movement is regular, systematic Bible study. Greasy-grace preachers focus on a few Scriptures and devote most of their time to philosophies of man they call "theology" from a few of their favorite teachers. But the falsehood of these teachers' pet doctrines is quickly exposed under the light of the sincere study of the Scriptures.

HOW TO DETOX FROM A SPIRITUAL DIET OF GREASY GRACE

My most urgent recommendation for people under this wrong teaching is to detox from it by starting to read the Bible daily. Start with the New Testament, reading two chapters a day and underlining any Scriptures that speak to you. Find an accountability partner who can keep you on track and discuss difficult passages with you. Read commentaries when you have time, and use the Greek-English interlinear texts to better understand the deeper meaning of words in the original language. There are two hundred and sixty chapters in the New Testament, so it will take you one hundred and thirty days to do that. I recommend reading the New Testament twice before reading the Old. Maybe three times is better, but you need to be well versed in the New before you can really understand the Old.

Don't pick and choose verses to support any previously held positions, but rather read through it all, letting the Scriptures speak to you and confront your previously held beliefs, ideas, and biases. Let the words challenge you and change you, rather than attempting to alter and use the Word of God for your own purposes.

When you do this, your faith will grow, and you will be able to answer those who seek to send false teachings your way. It is a lifelong pursuit; it is not a rush job, so take your time. Have honest discussions with people who have studied more than you. Be open to changing your views and even your moral stance when they conflict with the Word.

Most important, be consistently growing your faith by daily reading the Bible and applying its truths to your life. If you do this, your faith will not die; it will grow. Unbelief will shrink, and you will understand God more while drawing closer to Him.

FREEDOM FROM GREASY GRACE:
A TESTIMONY OF DETOX

I once was ministering at a series of meetings in Canberra, Australia, speaking about sacrifice, paying the price, and giving our all for the gospel. The messages included other topics, such as fasting and praying, personal discipline, seeking the Lord daily, giving sacrificially, and other practices of those who have accepted the costs of following the Lord.

There were moments of significant breakthroughs during these meetings. One man who had been experiencing financial problems decided to give sacrificially during the meetings, and within a few days, he had thirty thousand dollars of a debt canceled. People received healings in their bodies, and some such healings were dramatic. One woman in her early twenties had a brain tumor, and her healing was medically verified with brain scans from before and after. A large organization emailed that testimony to around eighty thousand people. What God did in those meetings went around the world. To God be all the glory, great things He has done.

Several people surrendered their lives to Christ. One particular night there was such a breakthrough in worship that we stayed singing in God's presence for more than two hours, and it seemed like only a short time. Several came before the meetings to tarry in prayer at the altar for hours before the service. We went to the shopping malls and other places and invited people to come. There were beautiful moments of overcoming, salvation, healing, and God's presence.

After several days of meetings, a young couple approached me. The woman spoke, her facial expression showing a combination of angst and gratitude. She explained that she and her husband were part of a ministry that was a vocal proponent of cheap grace. Their pastor taught that every Christian discipline was "religious" and "Pharisaical," a "man-made" attempt to reach God or please Him. This man taught that people didn't need to fast and pray, because "Jesus paid it all." Therefore, he concluded, Christians did not need to engage in anything requiring effort or causing personal difficulty. He taught a cotton-candy gospel—one that titillates to some measure when you initially eat of it but later causes tangible corruption to the heart.

This couple was suffering from the aftereffects of spiritual cotton-candy consumption. As we talked, the woman explained that they had been around this pastor's ministry for some time and had even paid a deposit for an upcoming trip with him. "He taught us that we don't need to fast or pray or press in, in any way," she told me. "He teaches that such things are 'striving' and from 'man-made' religion. At first, we loved the feeling of freedom that having no discipline or efforts brought. It sounded right in our heads; it sounded like grace! What an amazing revelation.

"After some time, deep within, we knew something wasn't right," she continued. "We had a nagging feeling that said something was off. Then we came to your meetings, felt God's presence, and heard your teaching. We saw in Scripture that [our pastor] is off track. But your teaching has restored us to a right relationship with God. We know the difference between false grace and true grace now. We are set free. We felt clean inside and canceled our trip to India. Now we will start to follow more biblical, Spirit-led models. Most of all, we feel free inside. We knew at a deeper level and through the study of Scripture that something was off, but now we know exactly what it is. God does require things of us. We can cooperate with grace and become who we are called to be. Jesus said we must take up *our* cross and follow Him. Thank you so much for telling the hard truth, David, because the Bible says the truth will set you free. Well, we are free!"

The couple's countenance had changed. They had truly detoxed from the false gospel of greasy grace. People who walk in this false revelation look like people who put on an insincere smile, but, below the thin veneer, a discerning person can see the troubled waters below the surface. This couple was no different. I'm so glad they got free.

When someone subscribes to the message of false grace, they almost always wear the mandatory pseudo-smile, a forced-looking sign of "freedom," but a more careful look exposes their façade for what it is. These people aren't truly at peace. In many cases, they are struggling with substance abuse, perversion, and immorality because they've been assured that such practices are "covered by the blood" and they continue to wrestle with sin and its consequences. Fake smiles or not, their eyes betray them. They are not at peace. They want to be, and they pretend to be. They feel a responsibility to be because of their beliefs. It's like trying to hold multiple beach balls beneath the surface of the water in a swimming pool. You can only hold down so many for so long before one forces its way to the surface. Eventually, the carnality that led them to the cheap-grace doctrine in the first place will be exposed.

I'm so grateful that this couple managed to detox and distance themselves from one of the most destructive heresies of our time. My prayer is that the same will happen in your life and the lives of anyone you may know who has fallen prey to the same trap. There is grace available to all—true, lavish grace. This grace doesn't make cheap excuses for sin; it *transforms* and *delivers* us from sin.

Get free from greasy grace today and jump into the new-found freedom of true grace that brings new life!

10

AGENDAS AND AUDIENCES

This book will keep you from sin,
or sin will keep you from this book.
—Inscription in the Bible belonging to John Bunyan,
author of *The Pilgrim's Progress*[22]

A wise person should have money in their head,
but not in their heart.
—Jonathan Swift

Underneath every false doctrine is a hidden agenda, a work of the enemy, a sinister plan. Lies come as a scheme to fool the listener. The cheese in a mousetrap isn't free. It looks free, it looks nice, but it's a trap. Greasy grace is no different.

22. Acacia John Bunyan Online Library, http://acacia.pair.com/Acacia.John. Bunyan/About.This.Site.html.

As we have discussed, many of those who embrace the greasy-grace doctrine do it for popularity; they want to feel enlightened and sell books. They want to look "progressive" or "friendly," and this agenda doesn't have room for the "less attractive" parts of the gospel. The challenging and seemingly harsh parts, the painful truths, are just too troublesome for what they try to portray. They're bad for business.

Jesus didn't build His ministry on such carnality. He intentionally "thinned the herd." Jesus knew He had insincere followers. Many times He spoke to the masses, but many people in the crowd without true devotion were not His purpose. He wasn't trying to build an email list or fan base. He gave His efforts to release a kingdom that would have God's will be done on earth as it is in heaven. Those who were attracted to Jesus for the wrong reasons would quickly flee at the sign of trouble. They do the same to this day.

OFFEND THE MIND TO REVEAL THE HEART

While teaching in the synagogue in Capernaum, Jesus explained, "Unless you eat the flesh of the Son of Man and drink His blood, you have no life in you." (See John 6:48–58.) Such a teaching would have been almost unimaginably offensive to His hearers. For the typical Jewish listener, this was more than they could take. Jesus knew how to fill an arena—and He knew how to empty one. A sure way to lose a Jewish audience is to start talking about drinking human blood and eating human flesh. Such notions were intolerable. If Jewish law forbade believers to be in the presence of a dead body or a menstruating woman, it certainly wouldn't have come remotely close to approving such practices as eating flesh and drinking blood. It was out of the question—completely offensive.

The thing is, God often intentionally offends the mind to reveal the heart. The heart of the elder brother was unmasked when the prodigal son returned. He wasn't happy to gain his brother back home or to see his father's joy restored. He was bitter because his younger brother had lived in sin and "gotten away with it" while he himself had never stopped following the rules.

GOD OFTEN INTENTIONALLY OFFENDS THE MIND TO REVEAL THE HEART.

Similar to many churchgoing people today, his actions were good, but his heart was wrong. The activities of the younger brother exposed the evil in his older brother's heart. That which offends us shows a lot about who we are internally. What we can't tolerate, move past, or see beyond will limit us.

When Jesus told the crowd of the necessity of eating His flesh and drinking His blood, many were offended and went away, never to return. Such people were following Jesus for the wrong reasons, and Jesus knew it. That is why He thinned the herd. He did not want a crowd with wrong motivations, so He offended the multitude so much that only the sincere stayed with Him and kept listening. The ones who remained still had many questions, but they were there for the right reasons—they desired a relationship with God, life's ultimate goal.

THE MURKY MOTIVES OF GREASY-GRACE PREACHERS

Some preachers and pastors want to accumulate as many followers as they can get—a goal that can't be reached by purposefully offending people. Such preachers often measure their value by the number of people in the pews and the amount of money in the bank, and they do whatever is needed to keep hindquarters in the pews and the offering buckets full. It is the flesh, and its corruption is a fruit that will not remain.

Still, popularity and acceptance are an obvious motivation of many preachers of the greasy-grace gospel. Someone who tells people trapped in sin that their behavior is no problem because "Jesus paid it all" will undoubtedly be popular here on earth, but the opposite will be true in the hereafter. For the greasy-grace preacher, you can have your sin cake and eat it, too.

Another motivation is what I call "kind heart and soft head." These are the well-intentioned preachers who simply don't know any better. They haven't studied the Scriptures enough or drawn near enough to the Lord to have an adequate understanding of the truth. This "zeal without knowledge" crowd is susceptible to the wolves in sheep's clothing mentioned above. They hear the argument "Jesus paid it all," which they call the "finished works." In their eyes, Jesus loves people no matter what they do. It rings true with them because they don't have the Spirit of truth operating in their hearts. They can't see that these slogans are twisted versions of the truth. They are either nice people who are easily fooled or just people without discernment who feast on whatever they are fed. Either way, they are deceived.

They can't perceive that a twisted truth is no longer a truth. It is not necessarily an indictment on the heart. Often, these people's hearts are truly pure, and they want to love people or, at the very least, avoid judging people. To them, the greasy-grace doctrine seems the best pathway. It does have a "form" of godliness, even though it denies the power to transform. (See 2 Timothy 3:5–7.)

The third category of greasy-grace adherents are the preachers who want to hide behind a theology that lets them continue indulging in their sin of choice. To their credit, they don't want to be guilty of not practicing what they preach, so they conveniently argue that sin is inconsequential. "What you do doesn't matter," they insist, "because 'Jesus paid it all.'" When people try to pursue holiness, they label such effort as "works" and lash out with accusations: "How can you be so arrogant as to think you can add one thing to the work of salvation Jesus has done for you?" What they are really doing is excusing their own sinful habits.

To the initiated believer who has truly been baptized in the Spirit, this is just a cheap parlor trick, a transparent manipulation. However, to the new or unlearned believer, it can be a stumbling block, for sure.

If you observe members of this third category of greasy-grace preachers and their lifestyle, you will find that they have counted the cost but don't like the price. Instead of being honest and saying, "You know, a life of purity, fasting and prayer, obedience to God, and dying to self isn't worth it to me," they move the goalpost. Sounding like the serpent in the garden when he questioned Eve, "Did God really say…?" they ask, "Did God really say we cannot embrace perversion or use recreational drugs? Did God say we need to have integrity?"

Whether on social media or from the pulpit, I have often confronted and corrected people who are clearly following or forwarding the lie of cheap grace. I don't do this because I view myself as a theological policeman but because I have seen the damage these lies can do. As a ministry leader, I have the heart to guard the sheep against the deceptive messages of these sweet-sounding wolves. I do this because people have come to me sharing how they have been set free from this kind of bondage.

While I am happy for them, I wonder how many will continue living in ignorance and die without being set free. I do this because some unwitting followers of greasy grace earnestly desire the truth. They don't know enough Scripture or aren't close enough with the Holy Spirit, so they cannot judge for themselves. I do this because what is inside me is the Spirit of truth, which cannot stand lies, especially sweet-sounding, religious lies. These are God's biggest enemies.

THE PROFIT MOTIVE OF CHEAP GRACE

In today's "pick and choose," spiritual but not religious environment, there is a temptation for teachers, ministers, and preachers to be selective in which parts of the Bible they preach. But faithful stewards of the Scriptures embrace the whole counsel of God. Be wary of a teacher or preacher who focuses on one thing because they will likely become unbalanced. Some people focus more on one thing because it's their passion, for various reasons and motives. This passion can sometimes lead to error.

As harsh a critic of the greasy-grace movement as I am, I do contend there is a continuum of greasy grace that runs on the low side of error, by applying God's mercy in places the Bible doesn't, to the top of the field, where preachers fabricate doctrine that sounds correct. I think some people have a touch of greasy grace, yet their hearts are in the right place. All they need is a better understanding of the Bible from a good teacher, and they will be fine. They want to walk in truth and fulfill God's will, but they just haven't been taught properly.

However, the group high on the scale of greasiness is either blissfully ignorant or willfully distorting God's Word. This realm is occupied mostly by "teachers" who deliberately distort God's Word and their blissfully ill-informed followers. These kinds of preachers say there is no hell when Jesus says there is. They say there is no need for repentance when Jesus says there is. They say that you don't need to do anything to be a Christian, and you can live however you want, when Jesus taught the opposite. Members of this high level of false teaching usually have an agenda.

As we discussed before, much of the greasy-grace doctrine is cultural. We live in the time of the mighty snowflake, the pampered baby whose highest priorities are avoiding judging, coddling emotions, and being "nice." Such goals are very destructive to our society because the masculine strength that has always accompanied feminine strength is diminished. It leads to cracks in the foundation of who we are as a people.

Enter the opportunistic preacher, teacher, or self-appointed "wise one." They aren't the same as those spoilsport, old-fashioned, narrow-minded teachers. They say, "Yes, I know, Jesus said a few 'uncool' things in the Bible, but we will wiggle and worm our way out of that and give you cotton candy instead of meat." Not always, but often, their motivation is simply profit. When you go against popular culture, you risk hurting your book sales.

HOW TO BE RELEVANT WITHOUT COMPROMISING BIBLICAL INTEGRITY

As ministers and people of faith, let's do everything we can to be relevant, engaging, answer honest questions, and adapt to the hearer of our day as best we can. Jesus related well to people, like the tax collectors and other sinners gathered around Him. He was intriguing and interesting. People felt convicted, for sure, and many repented; but with the truth, Jesus brought love and insight. They knew there was something special about Him, much different from the other teachers of the law. People from all walks of life could relate to Him, which was great. Sharing the good news of the gospel that is contextually relevant is highly beneficial. That being said, while the approach can change, the essentials of the message must not. "Yes" must not become "no," or "no" become "yes," simply for the sake of "reaching people."

I remember hearing about Chuck Smith, who founded and pastored Calvary Chapel in Southern California during the so-called "Jesus Movement" of the 1960s. Many of his congregants embraced the swell of young people coming to his church—a lot of them "hippies" with questionable hygienic habits and a tendency to go barefoot. Such habits offended other congregants, some of whom got together and posted a sign that read "No bare feet allowed" in an effort to protect the new sanctuary carpeting. At a board meeting, Chuck Smith made an appeal for leniency.

> "We will love these kids and teach them God's Word," Chuck challenged the leaders of the fellowship.... They had already taught the new believers James 2:1–4, he pointed out: *My brethren, do not hold the faith of our Lord Jesus Christ, the Lord of glory, with partiality. For if there should come into your assembly a man with gold rings, in fine apparel, and there should also come in a poor man in filthy clothes, and you pay attention to the one wearing the fine clothes...have you not shown partiality among*

*yourselves, and become judges with evil thoughts?...*How could the church discriminate against the shoeless and shower-less, Chuck asked, after teaching them that Scripture?[23]

Soon hordes of hippies started coming to Jesus. They still had long hair and smelled, but they wanted to hear about Jesus. The board capitulated, and Chuck Smith, his wife, Kay, and those working with them led thousands to the Lord in a movement that would spread the world over.

The key takeaway is that Chuck didn't change the message to suit his hearers; he changed church policy to include them. Wearing shoes and showering had previously been the accepted protocol, but in the Jesus Movement, they were optional. Before, sitting on pews was the norm; these hippie types liked to sit on the floor. Adjustments were made to accommodate their culture, but the church remained faithful to the true message of the gospel. They didn't change it to get more hearers; they stuck with the truth and amended their approach.

The worst of those who promote the greasy-grace doctrine do so to get more hearers and, subsequently, more money. For many preachers of the snowflake gospel, the reason for selling cheap grace is simply good old-fashioned profit. People want to be told they are okay when they are not and are willing to pay for someone to tell them that. It is the worst of the cheap-grace camp who are hired hands teaching strictly on this basis.

---

23. Jessica Russell, Debra Smith, and Tom Price, "They Called It the Jesus Movement—Part 1," Remembering Chuck Smith, *Calvary Chapel Magazine*, January 20, 2022, https://www.calvarychapelmagazine.org/word-press/remembering-pastor-chuck-smith-the-jesus-movement-part-1/.

GREASY-GRACE VERSUS SEEKER-SENSITIVE

The question has been raised, "Is greasy-grace doctrine the same as the seeker-sensitive movement?" My answer would be yes and no. Many seeker-sensitive churches refuse to talk about confrontational or controversial issues. They won't speak of hell or broach the subject of repentance, and they won't talk about sexual perversion and sin. And many will not talk about spiritual gifts.

Churches that can be labeled "seeker-sensitive" compose a huge category. Some of the "mainline," evangelical, Bible-believing churches that love God and teach sound doctrine could be described as seeker-sensitive churches. These churches may be right in many ways while still being incomplete. If I say that Jesus loves you and has a plan for your life, that is right. But if that is all I say, it is incomplete. It's not heresy; it's just a good doctrine needing to be further developed.

In the circles I travel in, "seeker-sensitive" is a dirty word. Many people view seeker-sensitive churches as telling half-truths or being more worried about filling pews than maturing the saints who sit in them. Some of these criticisms may be merited, but many of these churches intentionally focus on reaching the lost. High on their priority list, and rightly so, is winning souls for the kingdom of God. They value preaching the gospel, longing to communicate the gift of salvation of one's soul for whom Jesus died. It is a significant focus and foundational to any church or movement, but we must go deeper in the Lord.

I have seen the Lord use seeker-sensitive churches as a beginning stage of faith for multitudes. They might not go as "deep," but they cast a wide net, often bringing in a mighty harvest. All

I can say is, "Awesome!" Sadly, many of the converts in seeker-sensitive churches do not keep with the faith. The Word in their life is like seed sown on the rocky path, and though they are excited awhile, their enthusiasm quickly dies off because their roots lack depth. (See, for example, Matthew 13:19–23.)

DIVING BOARDS TO GO DEEPER

Others stay at that same shallow end of the pool where they were born again, but they do not grow much more. However, many serve there faithfully, bringing others into the fold. Still others get saved in that environment, and then their spirit longs for more. They have a yearning for a deeper place in Christ, and, as deep cries unto deep, they seek God for more of His Holy Spirit, as the Scripture demands. (See Psalm 42:7.)

Eventually, a friend will invite them to a meeting where believers are "swimming" in a deeper river. When they launch into the "more" that God has for them, they may receive the baptism in the Holy Spirit and may discover their gifts. If they keep pursuing the Lord, they will find a calling into ministry at some level. Only God knows what He can do with a person who is truly devoted to Him. There is no limit, except God's will, which is endless.

When that person has embraced God's plan for their life and walked with Him closely, they can thank God for that new church. They received prophecies there, the gifts of the wonderful Holy Spirit, and heard teaching at a deeper level than they ever knew. Yet, they still cannot forget where the gospel seeds were first sown in their heart.

Down at the seeker-sensitive church, where nothing too fancy or seemingly spiritual is going on, the waters of the new birth broke, and they received Jesus. Sure, later on, they embraced the fullness of the Spirit and the deeper things of God, leaving the milk for the meat of the Word. But they would never have gotten to the meat if they hadn't had the milk. (See Hebrews 5:12–14.)

So, God honors the hearts of the seeker-sensitive churches because they care enough for the seeker that they prepare a table from where he could eat. It is a glorious work. We should praise God for how the Lord uses the seeker-sensitive churches, initiating the gospel in people's hearts.

Sometimes, we Pentecostals and Charismatics are so "weird" that people cannot relate to us. Our weirdness is the result of our being deeply spiritual, of God doing something new and fresh and different in our midst. At other times, we are weird because we are weird. But I see our movement maturing, growing, and reflecting God in a better fashion. Even so, we are not without our flaws. We should humble ourselves and give thanks to those who focus on evangelism, winning the lost, and setting the table in a way that people can relate to when they come to feast on the things of the Lord.

COMPARING THE TWO

The seeker-sensitive group you just read about is vastly different from the greasy-grace movement. It is one thing to have your teaching incomplete, but advancing false teachings is vastly different. It applies especially to those whose teachings go against the Scriptures. Any teaching that says right is wrong, wrong is right, and Jesus didn't mean what He taught is just deception. Deceiving people with false doctrine is not the same as teaching an incomplete truth with a well-meaning heart.

When it comes to greasy grace and the seeker-sensitive movement, there is no comparison. The seeker-sensitive movement avoids things that some people aren't ready to hear yet. Jesus told His disciples, "I have more to tell you, but you don't have room to hear it (or bear it)." (See John 16:12.) There is a point where telling too much is too much. Jesus recognized this with His disciples.

People sometimes only have so much room to hear and understand. If someone has endured great suffering, they may be able to hear more, because the soil of their heart has been dug out by life so that a larger seed can be planted there. Still, this Jesus and Bible stuff, and the spiritual things are a bit new for many people. They don't have room to take it all in. A newborn can't eat a ham sandwich or try tip steak; he has to drink milk until he's ready for solid food.

People are similar because they have only so much room in their hearts. The seeker-sensitive folks meet them where they are, and the hungry pursue God at increasingly higher levels and seek greater depth as time goes by. It's a wise strategy. But the agenda and audience of greasy-grace and seeker-sensitive preaching is vastly different.

CONCLUSION:
A GOSPEL ABOUT NOTHING...
OR EVERYTHING

*Cheap grace...amounts to a denial of the living
Word of God, in fact, a denial of the Incarnation of the
Word of God. Cheap grace means the justification of sin
without the justification of the sinner.
Grace alone does everything, they say, and so everything
can remain as it was before.*
—Dietrich Bonhoeffer[24]

For those who grew up in the 1990s, like I did, there was no way to avoid the amusing TV show *Seinfeld*. There was nothing like it before, nor has there been since. In this self-deprecating,

24. Bonhoeffer, *Cost of Discipleship*, 46.

art-imitating-life sitcom, Jerry Seinfeld played a comedian living in New York City—something he had been for a long time in real life.

As character George Costanza, played by Jason Alexander once professed, it was a show "about nothing."[25] There was no content, storyline, reason, or purpose; it was just a group of New York Jewish guys yukking it up, making their way through their pointless lives. Part of the charm was that they weren't trying to make any political or moral statements. Some people may consider the show to be just a comical commentary on the "meaninglessness or minutiae of life." Others might feel it's a reflection of the reality of their own experience. Either way, the program resonated with many viewers. It was simple, dumb fun, and pointlessness was the point. It was a show about nothing.

When Jesus's sacrifice on the cross is not a call to carry our cross but an excuse to live in the flesh, the gospel becomes a Seinfeldian "gospel" about nothing. As closet universalists (some not closeted, some are blatant), the greasy-grace preachers say there is no hell, no need to repent, no need to fast and pray. Such a message negates the need to preach. When there is no hell, no judgment, and no sin, there is no need for a gospel. Really, such a gospel is a gospel that doesn't address anything of importance. It is no longer "good news"; it's just hot air. It is cotton candy, Velveeta cheese, and *Seinfeld* rolled into one—a powerless, meaningless message.

Jesus told His first hearers, "Repent, for the kingdom of God is at hand." (See Matthew 3:2.) Today, His glorious Holy Spirit speaks the same message to and through men and women, calling people to repent. These preachers share our need to turn

---

25. *Seinfeld*, Episode 43, "The Pitch," 1992.

from evil, our need to follow Christ, the mandate of the believer to deny themselves and take up their cross.

Heaven and hell are real, and they last forever. The eternal judgment Jesus taught about is something we should do everything we can to avoid. Jesus healed the sick, cast out devils, and called people to turn from their sin.

The gospel of good news was the message that although the judgment is waiting for the unrepentant sinner, there is hope while we are still on this earth. That hope is in Jesus Christ. We access Jesus through faith. This faith leads us to repentance, to turn from evil, and to follow God.

Jesus preached the kingdom of heaven, and later His followers preached "Jesus Christ and Him crucified." (See 1 Corinthians 1:23.) Jesus's sacrifice stayed or held back the judgment of God for whoever would repent, believe in, and follow Him. This is salvation, and it is the gospel. You can know God, and you can be forgiven. There is hope in Jesus: salvation from sin, hell, and eternal judgment, and the chance to live and walk with God forever. This is the gospel about something.

The gospel about nothing, greasy grace, denies these truths and thereby becomes insignificant. Every year in the USA alone, about 3,700 churches close their doors, which is about three to four times the number of those open.[26] These are primarily churches that have been mainline denominational churches that have become "liberal."

They embrace all kinds of sin, like our greasy-grace crowd, allowing perversion and abominations to run wild; after all, "a

---

26. John Dart, "Church-Closing Rate Only One Percent: More 'Churning' Among Evangelicals," *The Christian Century*, May 6, 2008, https://www.christiancentury.org/article/2008-05/church-closing-rate-only-one-percent.

loving God wouldn't tell anyone they are wrong." They communicate a gospel about nothing. Not surprisingly, very few people want to come and hear of this nothingness. They can listen to messages about nothing on TV at home. When you say it's okay to do anything and everything, and God loves you just the way you are, there's no need to change, and it's hard to see the value of salvation from anything. The enemy has woven a clever tapestry of deception: tell them there is no hell, no punishment; they can do what they want. The next obvious conclusion is there is no need for a Savior.

Today, the churches of most Christian denominations have a fraction of the people they used to attract. In fact, studies show that while many nominal or half-hearted churches, also known as "moderate" or "progressive" churches, are closing in droves, there are some that are flourishing. What are called "intense religions" by sociologists are thriving.[27] The "intense religions" are expressions of faith when people are active, engaged, committed, and self-sacrificial.

When you tell people that God accepts all kinds of behavior and choices, people will ask, "Why should I go to church?" "Why should I tithe?" "Why should I make any effort at all?" After all, "Jesus paid it all." Out the window go the heart and soul of the gospel, the importance of the gospel, and the need for the gospel. Soon, the church doors are shut, and many destinies are stolen.

What is left is a meaningless gospel. It has no teeth and no purpose, and it will eventually have no people.

---

27. Landon Schnabel and Sean Bock, "The Persistent and Exceptional Intensity of American Religion: A Response to Recent Research," *Sociological Science*, November 27, 2017, https://www.sociologicalscience.com/download/vol-4/november/SocSci_v4_686to700.pdf.

THE TRUE GOSPEL: THE CROSS WE ARE CALLED TO CARRY

The reality is, it is hard to die to self. Some seasons we must go through to do the will of the Father are excruciating. And, like Jesus in the garden of Gethsemane, we might also be inclined to pray his prayer, "Father, if possible, may this cup be taken from me. Yet not as I will, but Your will be done." (See Matthew 26:39.) This passage is very moving and shows that even Jesus wrestled with doing the Father's will over His own.

Sure, Jesus and the Father were one, but Jesus still had to live a life in human form. It's not easy. In my twenty-plus years of ministry, I have known people who have gone through very difficult things to do God's will. They have had to forgive people who had done heinous acts. They have had to obey God, even when it meant giving up everything to serve as a missionary in a foreign land. Some have gone through personal healing and in that process had to face the people that had done horrible things to them and vice versa. The cross we are called to carry is not an easy one. That is why it is called a cross.

> **THE CROSS WE ARE CALLED TO CARRY IS NOT AN EASY ONE. THAT IS WHY IT IS CALLED A CROSS.**

Because it is so hard, many opt out. They have a form of godliness but deny its power. (See 2 Timothy 3:5.) They like God's benefits, but when it is time to drink the cup, they make theological arguments as to why doing so is unnecessary. In a nutshell, greasy grace passes over the cup of what God wants so they can do what they want. It's a carnal, fleshly approach to following God. It's not genuine Christianity.

Romans 8:7 says that the carnal, fleshly, worldly mind is hostile to God. The King James Version puts it this way: "*The carnal mind is enmity against God.*" The basic understanding is they are enemies, even hated enemies. The carnal mind, the one that wants to live for the sensual and ungodly pleasures of this world, is hostile, angry, filled with hatred, and an enemy of God. So, this battle rages within us. Our flesh is at war with the God we love. It's not for the fainthearted.

This battle, like all battles, causes discomfort, like an internal wrestling match. If we do not renew our minds, the conflict will be more troublesome. Horrible cycles of guilt, shame, resentment, even bitterness can appear if we do not die the proper death to our carnal thinking. It's also hard to know what things must die. God's will is not always clear, and we sometimes second-guess ourselves. The life of a committed believer can be rough, but it's always worth it.

A life given over to the will of God is challenging, but it has great rewards. When we discipline ourselves, deny our flesh, and die the deaths we are called to die, then the Lord comes closer, and He is able to trust us more. As our fellowship grows deeper, we can step into God's plan for our lives.

What if, when Jesus was in the garden of Gethsemane, He had decided that a "loving God" wouldn't want Him to die on the cross? That it is "just not in God's character to allow us to suffer and hurt." After all, a loving father cares for his kids, wants the best for them, and isn't the heavenly Father equally caring? God is a God of love and grace, but how could He be asking me to do this, to die this death? That's not love, right?

Jesus could have reasoned His way off the cross, as many greasy-gracers do today. He could have talked Himself out of it, adopting a more "inclusive" theology, but He didn't. Jesus died to His own will and took the combination of the pleasure and joy that comes from following God. He didn't sell out, compromise, or make theological excuses for why He didn't need to do what God said was required. He died on a cross and willingly gave His life, and His reward was eternal life. Two thousand years later, His movement is still growing, and His sacrifice still changes lives every day. In the garden, that lonely moment, the dark moment, followed by His submission to God's will, forever changed human history.

He was our example to follow. He had choices to make, to choose life or death, to choose the Father's way or His way. So too we have options. We can choose carnality or a life in the Spirit. Today everyone still has that same choice: come down off the cross and have an "expanded" view of God's grace, or die to self. Jesus made the right choice; now it is our time to choose.

ABOUT THE AUTHOR

David Tomberlin is the president of David Tomberlin Ministries. Based in Southern California, his ministry has a heart for salvation of the lost and revival for the church.

David loves the ministry of the Holy Spirit and enjoys preaching the Word of God with miracles, signs, and wonders following. Many people have experienced healings and breakthroughs after receiving a word of knowledge from David.

He has been featured on Sid Roth's *It's Supernatural!* God TV, Daystar, and TBN's *Praise the Lord* program. After a supernatural encounter with the Lord at age twenty-one, David felt called to preach the gospel. He immediately began sharing the good news with people after that encounter.

To date, David has traveled to more than 60 nations, preaching the gospel, moving in miracles, and serving the poor while making every effort to lift high the name of Jesus.

David earned a bachelor's degree in business administration from Dallas Baptist University, two master's degrees from Fuller Theological Seminary in Pasadena, California, and an honorary doctorate from the University of Saint Thomas in Jacksonville, Florida. He coauthored *Amazed by the Power of God* with Bill Johnson, Randy Clark, and others.

David lives in Orange County, California, with his wife, Kate, and their four daughters, Christine, Emily, Rachel, and Farina.

Welcome to Our House!

We Have a Special Gift for You

It is our privilege and pleasure to share in your love of Christian books. We are committed to bringing you authors and books that feed, challenge, and enrich your faith.

To show our appreciation, we invite you to sign up to receive a specially selected **Reader Appreciation Gift**, with our compliments. Just go to the Web address at the bottom of this page.

God bless you as you seek a deeper walk with Him!

WE HAVE A GIFT FOR YOU. VISIT:

whpub.me/nonfictionthx

WHITAKER
HOUSE